D0935067

ENGLISH LINGUISTICS
1500—1800

(A Collection of Facsimile Reprints)

Selected and Edited by

R. C. ALSTON

No. 361

THE SCOLAR PRESS LIMITED
MENSTON, ENGLAND
1972

CHRISTOPHER WASE

METHODI PRACTICAE SPECIMEN

1660

A Scolar Press Facsimile

THE SCOLAR PRESS LIMITED
MENSTON, ENGLAND
1972

THE SCOLAR PRESS LIMITED
20 Main Street, Menston, Yorkshire, England

~~H 20~~
~~E 58~~
~~no. 361~~

ISBN 0 85417 886 4

PA 2084
W35
1972

Printed in Great Britain by
The Scolar Press Limited
Menston, Yorkshire, England

NOTE

Reproduced (original size) from the unique copy in the British Museum, by permission of the Trustees. Shelf-mark: E. 1750(2).

Christopher Wase was appointed headmaster of Dedham Royal Free School in 1655 and the work reproduced here was probably intended for use in the school. Wase subscribed to the ideas of educational reform put forward by Jan Amos Comenius (see nos. 143, 222 and 250 in this series) whose influence is obviously present in *Methodi practicae specimen* and whom Wase acknowledges in the opening sentences of the book: 'that great Regulator of *School-Policy*, who hath much matured the learning of *Tongues*, the Reverend and Singularly Ingenious *Comenius*' (sig. A 2 recto).

Wase's aim was to simplify the teaching of Latin by concentrating on the necessary minimum of grammar, and introducing the students to Latin literature as soon as these basic principles had been mastered. Judging by the number of subsequent editions the work was very successful. Editions appeared as follows: 1663, 1667 ('Fifth edition'), 1669 ('Fifth edition'), 1676 ('Seventh edition'), 1682 ('Eighth edition'), 1690 ('Ninth edition'), 1709 ('Twelfth edition'), 1731 ('Twelfth edition'); there is also an entry in the ledger of the printer Charles Ackers for 2,000 copies on 27th November 1744, but no copy of the book appears to have survived.

A further work by Wase on education is *Considerations concerning Free Schools*, 1678; he was also the compiler of an English-Latin, Latin-English dictionary, *Dictionarium minus*, 1662 (Part 2 is dated 1661).

Reference: Wing W 1019.

J. R. TURNER

MAR 20 1974

Methodi Practicæ Specimen. 1887

A N
ESSAY
OF A
PRACTICAL GRAMMAR;
OR
An Enquiry after a more eafie
and certain help to the *Conftruing*
and *Pearfing* of AUTHORS; and to
the making and fpeaking of *Latine*.

Containing a *Set of Latines* anfwer-
able to the moft Fundamental *Rules of Grammar*,
and delivered in an eafie Method for the firft beginners to make *Latine*, at their entrance on the
Rules of Conftruction.

By *Chriftopher Wafe*, M. A.
Teacher of the Free-School of Q. *Eliza-
beth* at *Dedham* in *Effex*.

——— *Quantum vertice ad auras.*
Ætherias, tantum radice in Tartara tendit.
October.

London, Printed by D. *Maxwel*, and are to be fold
by *Charls Adams* at the Talbot in Fleetftreet. 1660.

TO THE
READER.

I T muſt not be denied, That the preſent Age hath brought to light, great helps to the Inſtruction of *Youth* in the *Latine Tongue :* For thoſe who in Forein parts have invented means for the expediting of this, it may ſuffice to inſtance in that great Regulator of *School-Policy*, who hath much matured the Learning of *Tongues*, the Reverend and Singularly Ingenious *Comenius*. At home divers happy pieces have been publiſhed; with all which, it might farther conduce to the faciliating that employment, if the work of making *Latine* were put into an orderly and artificial courſe : Which ſeems to have been left too much at large, not with us onely, but in other parts, as far as I can underſtand. I hope it will be approved to the *Judicious Reader*, that this Labor is not unneceſſary, if he ſhall with me reflect,

I. That there are wholly wanting aſſiſtances of *Technical Books* which might draw on

Children

Children to the exercise, of the ſeveral or moſt principal operations of *Grammar* in train; for tranſlating out of the *Vulgar* into *Latine.* It would turn to better account, if, as the *Children* are intruſted with any ſtock, they were required to trade with it; and were directed orderly to refund it in practiſe.

II. That it is more difficult to learn the Reaſon of the *Latine Tongue* by pearſing of *Authors,* then by making *Latines*; the Inveſtigation of the *Theam* from the *Obliques,* being far more various then the deſcending from the *Theam* to the *Obliques* by certain and uniform *Characteriſticks.*

III. That it is evident by an *Induction* of the ſeveral *Arts,* amidſt which we converſe: That as without the direction of a *Maſter,* it is difficult by bare practiſe to arrive to the perfection or truth of *Art:* So neither is it much riddance, if a *Maſter* ſhould couch in writing the ſeveral operations of his whole *Art,* and exact of his *Novice,* to commit it all to memory, an end, before he fall to practiſe any particulars of it, and thereby to underſtand them: But the moſt eaſie, ſpeedy, and familiar way is, after very ſhort, general Inſtructions, concerning the terms of that *Art* premitted, if the *Learner* put his hand to the work,

work; that particular *Problemes* be laid down in a clear direction; this followed with manifold working, that reviewed and poliſhed with continual correction. Thus the *underſtanding* will run parallel with the *memory*; for we then onely know a rule of working, when we can do the work.

IV. To diſtribute *Grammar* into *Problemes*, makes it more comprehenſible to a narrow-ſighted *underſtanding*, and more portable for the weak *memory* of a *Childe*; that *ſtrength* may in a convenient time remove a Sack of Corn into a Store-houſe, if it be parcelled into proportionable burthens; which can in no time carry it away, by heaving to lift at once, that which is a burden over-proportioned to it.

V. This may be ſome defence for the ſeeming *compaſs* that this *method* carries the *Learner* about; for the attainment of *Arts* and *Sciences*, is well compared to the climbing a ſteep Hill. Our *fancy* may contrive to ſpring up perpendicularly, but it will be found the moſt feaſible and eaſie way to gain the top by a ſpiral aſcent.

VI. Hereby different *capacities* are comprehended, quicker *apprehenſions* will be informed and confirmed, and brought to a habit of ready working; while the ſlower are not

A 3 diſdifcouraged, nor wholly left behinde : Some wits are of a more yielding, others of a more fturdy matter. Now each fingle inftance propounded to be wrought, is as a knock of a Hammer, to rivet into the *underftanding* and *memory*, that rule, upon which it depends in the working : And the feveral heads of *fenfe* ferve the more to clench it down.

VII. Nor is it any *real compafs* that this *method* takes more than others, if we confider the perpetual *parts* and *repetitions* ufed in learning the *Grammar* ; for to work by the fame *rule* in forty examples, is lefs tedious both to *Mafter* and *Scholar*, and makes more to the underftanding that *rule*, and is not longer then to repeat and hear the *rule* forty times over.

VIII. Yet becaufe *wits* are not of equal acutenefs, and fome do more readily apprehend the propounded *rule* than others can. If a *fingle pupil* be inftructed, when he fufficiently perceives the operation, and the particular *cafes* of it are falved, it matters not, that he be detained to pafs through all thofe proofs, that are here offered (which yet would be not without profit to him) but he may fpeed on to the following *Fundamental Canons*, and there will be no abruptnefs in fuch proceeding onely, if the *rule* be carried before in the *underftanding* ;

ſtanding ; the beſt expedition for *Forms* is, that upon diſcovery of differing parts they be not unequally matched : So that the prudence of the *Maſter* may make it neither too long, for the more *quick*, nor too ſhort, for the more *ſlow*. And as the received *method* is a means to diſcover the inequality of *memories*, ſo this will be helpful to try the quickneſs of apprehenſions.

IX. That the *examples* are not very coherent, not claſſical, but plain, and the way hath ſomewhat of new in it ; theſe ſeveral *objections* admit a diſtinct ſolution, not very difficult to be found out ; the firſt onely muſt be excuſed, the latter three defended and owned. Indeed it were to be approved, that beſides the truth of Rule, a conſtant harmony of Senſe might run through the whole body of *examples* in the Art : For then the minde would be leſs diſtracted, and dwell more willingly upon its work, and the intention of the inſtances more evident. If it be narrowly looked into, this hath been attempted in the preſent Scheam (however the difficulty of the matter, with the inability of the Author, may have occaſioned a coming ſhort of what may be in this point imagined and deſired,) ſo that a disjoyned conformity, and grateful variety, have been aim'd at in the whole ; the heads

of

of Senſe being drawn from the World, Natural, Artificial, or Moral: Neither are they
yet more unſuitable to one another, then the
examples, throughout the received *Grammar.*
Now that this might be effected, it was ſecondly proper to caſt a ſet of Sentences, rather then
to no advantage, ambitiouſly to collect them
from the Authors of Latine. Why muſt it
be ſtood upon to atteſt the conſtant and ordinary expreſſions of the Tongue from the pure
Writers? or what are *Tully, Seneca, Terence,
Virgil, Ovid,* to him that enters on his *Accidents?* Is not the Maſters authority to him
more known and more important? *Ariſtotle*
ſaith rightly, *The Learner muſt believe.* I have
herein aſſerted freedom to *Grammar,* which the
Writers of other Arts take to themſelves, and
Comenius the great advancer of *Didacticks* does
ordinarily challenge. Theſe were thirdly, cal-
culated for the weakeſt capacities of raw and
tender beginners to be familiar in Senſe and
Analogious (ordinarily) in conſtruction, and
laid even one by another in an orderly contexture, wherein nothing ſublime or profound,
nothing anomalous, nothing prepoſterous,
might trouble the yong Learner; and if this
be blamed, with as juſt reaſon may a Nurſe or
Mother be blamed, who ſhould remove out
of the way what-ever might be occaſion of
ſtumbling

stumbling to her childe that is upon practising to go alone. No ground is plain enough to preserve Children from knocks at that time, nor can any method be so clear, but Novices will at first be apt to mistake, till they be set upright; the charge must here lie rather after an information, whether it be plain enough. Fourthly, If upon an inquiry it appear to design somewhat unattempted hitherto by the several compilers of *Grammar*, whether at home or abroad, this will vindicate the Author from the imputation of a Pagiary: Indeed here is offered at an artificial Systeme of Vulgars (as some term them) or (exercises of Translation from the *Mother Tongue* into *Latine*; therefore by others from the opposite term called) *Latines* (as what they are to be made.) The whole care of this hath hitherto been left to the leasure of Masters, who are either put to the trouble of perpetual dictating Latines, proper to the proficiency of those Forms which they instruct, or else to put them to some English Author, and exact of them to translate tasks out of it; which is at once to lay the whole weight of the *Latine Grammar*, upon a beginners shoulders: We bring them to pearse *Latine*, by leading them through *Sententiæ Pueriles*, and *Pueriles Confabulatiunculæ*, and *Corderius Colloquies*, and so to *Esops Fables*,

Fables,, *Cato's Diſtichs*, *Terence*, and the eaſier pieces of *Ovid* and *Tully*. Ought not the ſame condeſcenſion to be uſed in requiring the Work from them ? Should they be at once, at the very firſt engaged upon the whole work of *Grammar* promiſcuouſly ? Allowing, that they have the whole body of *Grammar* in their memories; yet if they have it not in their underſtandings, it is but like a caſh committed to their keeping, locked up, they ſhould be accountable onely for ſo much, as is intruſted to them under their own Key: Now a ſingle *example* does very difficultly open to ſo yong beginners a general rule, but manifold practiſe ſliding from the Vulgar to the Latine Tongue, is a more certain and ready Key. And beſides this difficulty to the Learner, promiſcuous Latines are an inſufficient proof of *Grammar* skill: They are unequitable to the yong Student, and inadæquate to the work. Contingent practice cannot without a great tract of time, let one into a full knowledge of any Art, nor does it then certainly. Theſe two Reaſons may ſerve to maintain the Introduction of the *Latine Praxis* to be proved by the rule, concurrently with the Engliſh; by which *Analyſis* and *Geneſis* of *Latine*, it may become familiar to them to aſcend from the *Obliques*, to the *Theame*, and

to

to deſcend from the *Theam* to the *Obliques*, as a Seaman attains by Cuſtom to run up and down the Ladder of a Maſt, which would be difficult to one not practiſed to it: Nor is this method conſiderably differing from the received way in Schools; but onely a ſuperinducing of a farther help which may appear to have been wanting in carrying them on in the received Authors.

X. What I apprehend a more material Objection, is, That though my liberty in conceiving *examples* be allowed, though the way be granted pleaſant, becauſe more coherent than ordinary, eaſie, and ſo far new, as is not abhorrent from, but ſubſervient unto the received order of *Teaching :* Yet theſe proceedings, while they indulge the eaſe of the Learner, lead him by fallible way-marks, when he lanches into an Author; he ſhall not finde thoſe meaſured uniform Clauſes, thoſe entire Sentences, thoſe Analogous parts; another face of Oration will preſent it ſelf. He muſt engage with language in a ſtile different from the Engliſh compoſition. Which way will our yong practitioner in Latine, now turn himſelf? If the artificial and umbratile method ſail in encounters with natural language, it delights fairly; but inconveniences foreſeen are in a fair way to be prevented. The way-marks of the
Latine

Latine language, are the terminations of
Noun and Verb, principally with other accidents of the Tongue, which are more evi-
dently propounded, and rendred more familiar
by uſe in this method. The eaſineſs which a-
riſes from ſuiting the Clauſes under their Rule,
from giving entire Sentences, from picking
out *Regular Parts* of the Sentence, from put-
ting a compoſition commenſurate to the
known order of our Native Tongue, onely
prepare the Learner to be acquainted with,
and prompt in the Declenſions and Conjuga-
tions, by paſſing on without rubs. It hinders
not that a childe may grow up to travel in rug-
ged ways, who hath learned to ſet his ſteps
upon the ſmootheſt pavement, and from before whom, at firſt, all cauſes of ſtumbling
have been ſtudiouſly removed ; yet even this
formality is endeavored to be taken of, by
throwing ſeveral Sentences under their proper
Rule, into an arbitrary order in Verſes, by
ſubjoyning obſervations concerning the peculiar compoſition of the Latine Tongue, by
drawing up the Anomalies into a Synoptical
Table, by adviſing the Learner of the uſual
abridgements of Sentences (eſpecially when
he is carried on to look into the conſtruction
of Zeugmatical Periods) by ſumming up divers Rules into one Recapitulatory Practiſe
(whereby

(whereby thoſe contrived equalities fall off, and onely the Rule ſticks by.

XI. Now, though it be admitted, that this courſe is profitable to the Learner of *Latine*; it will not therefore follow, that a like innovation would be as uſeful in learning the Greek, becauſe there is a diſparity of Reaſon. This is taken up by Children, and thoſe wholly unacquainted with the Art of *Grammar*; that is ſuperadded to them grown more adult, and well verſed in the *Latine Grammar*, eſpecially when the Accidents of the *Latine* are far more incommenſurate to the Engliſh, then thoſe of *Greek* are to *Latine*.

XII. The onely Poſtulate of this Method is, that the Scholar be able to write; who ſhall do well to have a *Dictionary* of his own; and is further deſired to get a Paper-Book, wherein to enter his *Latines* fair after correction; that ſo he may have by him a *Sententiæ Pueriles*, which he may frequently read with underſtanding and delight, as being of his own making.

XIII. The deſired benefit of it is, that the induſtrious Student may underſtand *Grammar*; and with eaſe paſs on unto, and with ſpeed and profit paſs through the received Authors.

XIV. I finde by a Book newly publiſhed, and

and come to my hand, that a like deſign hath been contrived and ſucceſsfully practiſed by Mr. *Charls Hool.* I have reaſon to be much confirmed by the teſtimony of ſo worthy an Author; whom, though by face unknown, yet from his Tranſlations ſeen by me, and the Preface to *Cato's* Diſtichs, I have honored not onely as candid and induſtrious, but a-cutely judicious in Didacticks: Not that I ſhould paſs by his being experienced in Teaching, who was (as I collect from his *New Diſ-covery of the old Art of Teaching School*) a School-Maſter, before I was a School-Boy. In the laſt mentioned Book, *Page* 57, 58, alſo 118, 119, 120. his notion concerning ſuch like Scheam, and his progreſs and practiſe in it, are expreſt. I promiſe my ſelf, when I ſhall attain to ſee his pieces of this nature publiſh-ed, that the defects in this eſſay may be much redreſſed: And this my attempt may con-fer, if nothing of light or ſtrength to the work; yet the weight of a witneſs to the way.

XV. I can ſafely from experience teſtifie, concerning the one part of this Work, that is, the Train of Engliſhes to be done into La-tine, that hereby without much tediouſneſs, either of Scholat or Teacher, the attentive Learner, hath with ſpeed and eaſe been let in

to

To Epiſtle to the Reader.

to a ſteady skill of making Latine ; and to perceive with evidence, the contexture of the Latine ſtile. What is farther contributed hereto by the other Additionals, the Work not being publiſhed through want of Copies, I could not make tryal. The Reaſons of adding them, have been above mentioned.

ERRATA.

ERRATA.

Age 3. *for* Punier iemus, *read* Puniar emur. p. 6. *for* pleguntur *read* leguntur. p. 7. *for* oliva r. olivæ. p. 9. *for* censûs r. censûs. p. 14. *for* Haſtaratus r. Haſtatus. p. 18. *for* nudeus r. nucleus. p. 19. *for* præbe r. præbet. p. 20. *for* judiciem r. judicem. p. 24. *for* Foſſorm r. Foſſor, *for* adeſit r. madeſit. p. 30. *for* eſtimat r. æſtimat. p. 31. *for* Vertix īces r. Vertex īces, *line following*, *after* Vultus ûs, (*add*) *but* Manus, Acus, Tribus, Porticus, Domus, *and* Trees, *as* Quercus, Pinus, *are Feminine*; *and after* Facies ês, (*add*) Meridies, *is Singular and Maſculine*. Dies *Singular*, *is doubtful*, Plural *Maſculine*. p. 32. En r. ᵉEn. Danto r. ᵈDanto. Drando r. Grando. Clamys r. Chlamys, p. 34. accute r. accurate. p. 40. opperarius r. operarius. p. 41. acceſſit r. aceſcit. p. 44. *turning* er, è. *leave out* er, r. *turning* è. p. 46. *for* l. & r. *before* -ceo-geo, *make it* ſi, r. l. & r. *before* geo, & l. *before* ceo, *make it* ſi, p. 47. *for* But Incumbo, &c. *omit* in, *also* Intelligo, Aperio, Operio, ui. r. But -+cumbo, &c. *omit* m, *also* Aperio, Operio, ui. Intelligo, Diligo, Negligo exi. *Ten lines below*, *turn theſe three words* (*make* ſus *but*) *croſs the page*.

Tego

Tego, tegere Texi texiffe. *To cover.*

Sum effe Fui fuiffe. *To be.*
Poffum poffe Potui potuiffe. *To be able.*
Volo velle Volui voluiffe. *To will.*
Nolo nolle Nolui noluiffe. *To be unwilling.*
Malo malle Malui maluiffe. *To be more willing.*
Fero ferre Tuli tuliffe. *To bear.*

The Pre-ſent Tenſe.	Ego Tegis tegit	Tegimus Tegitis tegunt	Sum Es eft Eram *like* Texeram	Sumus Eftis funt
Imperfect.	Tegebam Tegebas tegebat	Tegebamus Tegebatis tegebant	Ero Eris erit	Erimus Eritis erunt
Future.	Tegam Teges teget	Tegemus Tegetis tegent	Poffum Potes poteft Poteram *like* Eram Potero	Poffumus Poteftis poffunt Ero
Perfect.	Texi Texifti texit	Teximus Texiftis texerunt	Volo Vis vult	Volumus Vultis volunt
Pluperfect.	Texeram Texeras texerat	Texeramus Texeratis texerant	Nolo Nonvis non vult Malo Mavis mavult	Nolumus Nonvultis nolunt Malumus Mavultis malunt
Near-Fu-ture.	Texero Texeris texerit	Texerimus Texeritis texerint	Fero Fers fert	Ferimus Fertis ferunt

The

The Subjunctive Mood is form'd from the conjugated Verb by this Rule :

Turn o *into* am ; *add* m.
Turn i *into* erim ; *add* m, *as from.*

Tego   Tegam. s. t. mus. tis. nt.
Tegere   Tegerem. *But* Sum, Possum, Volo, Nolo, Malo,
Texi   Texerim. *make* Sim, Possim, Velim, Nolim, Malim.
Texisse   Texissem.

This Mood is used with Particles which conjoyn Sentences, as ut uti, utinam ; ni, fi, nifi ; qued, cum. *The Present also forbids with* ne, *and bids being set by it self.*

The Imperative Mood is form'd from the Present redoubled, by casting away re, *or the last syllable; as*

Tegere Tege.

Tege   Tegite.   Dicere, Ducere, Facere, *cast away the*
Tegito   Tegitote.   *short* e *also; and from* Nolle *cometh*
tegito   tegunto.   Noli.   Noli ⎱Nolite ⎱
                   Nolito ⎰Nolitote ⎰

The Participles, Tegens *covering,* Tegendus *to be covered,* Tectus *covered,* Tecturus *about to cover. The three last of which are commonly joyned with* Sum.

The Passive Voice Tegor tegi.

Tegor   Tegimur   Tegar ⎱ris, tur,
Tegeris   Tegimini   Tegerer ⎰mur, mini. n tur.
tegitur   teguntur

Tegebar   Tegebamur   Tegere   Tegimini
Tegebaris   Tegebamini   Tegitor   Tegiminor
tegebatur   tegebantur   tegitor   teguntor

Tegar   Tegemur
Tegeris   Tegemini
tegetur   tegentur

(3)

The long Verb hath three Conjugations.

1. are.   2. ere *from* eo.   3. ire.

Laudo laudare	Laudavi laudavise.	*To praise.*
Moneo monere	Monui monuisse.	*To advise.*
Punio punire	Punivi punivisse.	*To punish.*

Laudo Laudamus	Moneo Monemus	Punio : imus
Laudas Laudatis	Mones Monetis	Punis : itis
laudat laudant	monet monent	punit : * iunt

* Eo &
Queo make
eunt &
queunt.
Ibam Qui-
bam.

Laudabam, Monebam, Puniebam, *like* Tegebam.

Laudabo Laudabimus	Monebo	Monebimus Puniam : iemus
Laudabis Laudabitis	Monebis	Monebitis Punies : ietis
laudabit laudabunt	monebit	monebunt puniet : ient

Ibo Qnibo.

Laudor Laudamur	Moneor	Monemur Punior : imur
Laudaris Laudamini	Moneris	Monemini Puniris : imini
laudatur laudantur	monetur	monentur punitur : iuntur

Laudabar, Monebar, Puniebar, *like* Tegebar.

Laudabor Laudabimur	Monebor	Monebimur Punier : iemus
Laudaberis Laudabimini	Moneberis	Monebimini Punieris : iemini
laudabitur laudabuntur	monebitur	monebuntur punietur : jentur

The *Subjunctive* Mood of the *first* of the *long* turns o *into*
em.
The *Imperative* Mood of the long *Verbs* keeps *their Vowel.*

Lauda Laudate	Mone	Monete Puni	Punite
Laudato Laudatote	Moneto	Monetote Punito	Punitote
laudato laudanto	moneto	monento punito *	puniunto

* Eunto &
queunto.

Laudare Laudamini	Monere	Monemini	Punire	Punimini
Laudator Laudaminor	Monetor	Moneminor	Punitor	Puniminor
laudator laudantor	monetor	monentor	punitor	puniuntor

B 2

A

A Noun is exprest as a Verb, with Number, Singular, and Plural.

An Eye, Eyes, Oculus, Oculi. *A Cheek, Cheeks,* Gena, Genæ.

An Ear, Ears, Auris, Aures. *A Lip, Lips,* Labrum, Labra.

From three Plurals ending in i, æ, s, *arise three Declensions.*

In each Declension we consider three places of the Noun in its sentence. The After-noun of, *the After-verb, the After-sentence to,* with.

i		æ		s	
Oculi	Oculorum	Genæ	Genarum	Auris	Aurium.
Oculum	Oculos	Genam	Genas	Aurem	Aures.
Oculo	Oculis	Genæ, â.	Genis	Auri, e.	Auribus.

There are also Plurals ending in a *which want the second Case.* A *from* um *is of the first declension :* A *not from* um *is of the third ; as* Labrum, Labra, *thus, but* Caput, Capita *otherwise,*

um		a				
Labri		Labrorum		Capitis		Capitum.
x x		x x		x x		x x
Labro		Labris		Capiti, e.		Capitibus.

There are also of the third in s *Nouns contracted in* ûs, *as* Vultus, Vultûs; *and in* ês, *as* Facies, Facies.

Vultûs.	Vultuum.	Faciei.	Facierum.
Vultum.	Vultus.	Faciem.	Facies.
Vultui, u.	Vultibus.	Faciei, e.	Faciebus.

PRAXIS,

PRAXIS I.

Nominative and Verb agree in Number.

AMnis fluit.	*The Rose withers.*
Torrens ruit.	*The blossom blasteth.*
Imber cadit.	*The flower fades.*
Fulmen vadit.	*The morning hasteth.*
Nix solvitur.	*The Sun sets.*
Æther volvitur.	*The shadow flies.*
Ros arescit.	*The Candle wastes.*
Vita vanescit.	*Man dyes.*

The Moon waxes.	Luna decrescit.
The Water flows.	Aqua refluit.
The Graß springs.	Herba marcescit.
The Winde blows.	Ventus reflat.

Rota versat.

Res fluit; ardet amor. Res defluit; alget amicus.
Sol micat, umbra patet. Sol cadit, umbra latet.

Culter secat.	*A Spade digs.*
Gladius necat.	*A Rake gathers.*
Cuneus findit.	*A Prong pitches.*
Securis scindit.	*A Sickle reaps.*
Virga cædit.	*A Saw cuts.*
Fustis lædit.	*A whetstone whets.*

Corrigiæ stringunt, tenet uncus, fibula nectit.
Fila suunt, figit subula, pungit acus.

Ager aratur.	*Wooll is spun.*
Gleba dimovetur.	*Yarn is weaved.*
Arvum sæpitur.	*Cloth is dyed.*
Fossa foditur.	*A Garment is sowed.*

Discitur ars, ædes fabricantur, quæritur esca.
Explorantur agri, Sollicitantur aquæ.

B 3

Irretitur avis, terretur cerva, feritur
Piscis, plantatur terra, rigatur olus.

Agnus nutritur, mulgetur vacca, putatur
Vitis, cæduntur ligna, domantur equi.

Carpuntur flores, refecantur prata, premuntur
Ceræ, conduntur mella, cremantur apes.

Tendentur lanæ, velluntur lina, pleguntur
Poma, seges metitur, contumulatur Homo.

A Burler twitches.	*A Cloth-worker furbishes.*
Knots are twitched.	*Garments are furbished.*
A Sherman sheers.	*A Dyer dies.*
Flocks are sheered.	*Cloths are dyed.*

Net netrix, Textor contexit, Mango resarcit.
Fullo lavat, vendit venditor, emptor emit.

Tornio tornat	Sartor sarcit.
Mensa tornatur	Vestes sarciuntur.
Victor viet	Sutor suit.
Dolia vientur	Calcei suuntur.
	Artifex operatur.

Cerdo suit, Faber ædificat, Crustarius albat.
vectat nauta, fodit fossor, arator arat.

The heart thinks.	Digitus indicat.
The task is thought.	Scriptum indicatur.
The eye sees.	Unguis scabit.
The Book is seen.	Caput scabitur.
The ear hears.	Manus tractat.
The Master is heard.	Pagina tractatur.
The Tongue whispers.	Pes ambulat.
The lesson is whispered.	Terra ambulatur.

Infans vagit, Homo loquitur, Vulpeculâ gannit.
Hinnit equus, mugit bucula, balat ovis.

PRAXIS.

PRAXIS II.

THe *Subſtantive Verbs* Sum, Fio; *and Paſſives* Dicor, Appellor *draw a Nominative after them.*

Suber eſt arbor.	*The Roſe is a flower.*
Spongia eſt alga.	*The Whale is a fiſh.*
Canna eſt arundo.	*The Lion is a beaſt.*
Ebur eſt dens.	*The Eagle is a bird.*
Membrana eſt pellis.	*Wine is a juice.*
Achates eſt lapis.	*A Date is a fruit.*

Lilia ſunt flores, baccæ dicuntur oliva.
Bellua balæna eſt, Vipera beſtiola eſt.

A trade is an eſtate.	Scholaris eſt apicula.
Labor is a treaſure.	Libri ſunt flores.
Meat is a refreſhment.	Schola eſt alveare.
Play is a recreation.	Sapientia eſt mel.
Sleep is reſt.	Ceſſator eſt fucus.

Ars eſt palma, Schola eſt ludus, Sunt arma libelli,
Præceptor dux eſt, Militia eſt ſtudium.

Obſerve I. *That the Latines delight to pack the Verb laſt, if the cloſure of Vowel and Conſonant in the beginning and end of words, or of both leſs harſh Conſonants permit, as* Suber arbor eſt : Achates lapis eſt. *So that if the Verb couple different numbers, as* Olera ſunt cibus : Boletus eſt deliciæ. *The Verb put laſt complies with the Nominative next before it, as* Olera cibus eſt. Boletus deliciæ ſunt. *Florum colores horti decus eſt.*

II. *That the Latines uſe frequently to leave out the Subſtantive Verb, eſpecially in Similitudes, as* Avis, navis; pectus, prora; venter, carina; alæ, remi; cauda, gubernaculum. *So* Homo, bulla; vita, ſpithama.

Covetouſneſs

Covetousneß is a vice. — Avaritia appellátur frugalitas.
Liberality is a vertue. — Liberalitas dicitur profusio.
Wealth is an help. — Temperantia vocatur austeritas
Poverty is an hindrance. — Ebrietas habetur hilaritas.
Lazineß is a sleep. — Clementia putatur lenitas.
Praise is a spur. — Disciplina nominatur asperitas.

Copia fit morbus, Paupertas est medicina:
Paupertas dolor est, fit medicina labor.

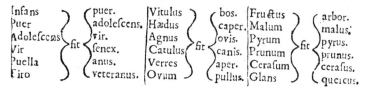

Infans		puer.	Vitulus		bos.	Fructus		arbor.
Puer		adolescens.	Hædus		caper.	Malum		malus.
Adolescens	fit	vir.	Agnus	fit	ovis.	Pyrum	fit	pyrus.
Vir		senex.	Catulus		canis.	Prunum		prunus.
Puella		anus.	Verres		aper.	Cerasum		cerasus.
Viro		veteranus.	Ovum		pullus.	Glans		quercus.

PRAXIS III.

OF (*after a Noun*) *is a token of the Genitive Case.*

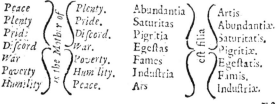

Juba		Equi.	Clusters		Vine.
Crista	est honor	Galli.	Flowers	are the ornament of the	Garden.
Cauda		Pavonis.	Oaks		Wood.
Apex		Upupæ.	Ships		River.

Est Rosa laus florum, Balæna est terror aquarum,
Est Leo rex pecudum. Dux avium est aquila.

Fax noctis Luna est, Titan est flamma Diei.
Est homo Rex mundi, Rex hominum Deus est.

Peace		Plenty.	Abundantia		Artis.
Plenty		Pride.	Saturitas		Abundantiæ.
Pride	is the Mother of	Discord.	Pigritia	est filia	Saturitatis.
Discord		War.	Egestas		Pigritiæ.
War		Poverty.	Fames		Egestatis.
Poverty		Humility.	Industria		Famis.
Humility		Peace.	Ars		Industriæ.

Est

Eſt cenſus nutrix hominum concordia. Fabri
Inſtrumenta juvant, Militis arma nocent.

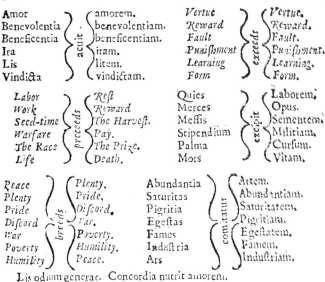

A contempt of {
Error
Money
Dangers
Pleaſures
} is the fruit of {
Prudence.
Juſtice.
Fortitude.
Temperance.
} | Amor {
Luſûs
Voluptatis
Lucri
Otii
} eſt labes {
pueritiæ.
adoleſcentiæ.
ſenectutis.
vitæ.
}

Flos perit ætatis, virtutis gemma pereanat.
Gemmæ durat honos, gloria floris abit.

Obſerve, *The Genitive is uſually put firſt in order, ſo is*
Terræ motus, Aquæductus.

PRAXIS IV.

A *Noun following a Verb, is of the Accuſative Caſe.*

Amor
Benevolentia
Beneficentia
Ira
Lis
Vindicta
} acuit {
amorem.
benevolentiam.
beneficentiam.
iram.
litem.
vindictam.

Vertue
Reward
Fault
Puniſhment
Learning
Form
} exceeds {
Vertue.
Reward.
Fault.
Puniſhment.
Learning.
Form.

Labor
Work
Seed-time
Warfare
The Race
Life
} proceeds {
Reſt
Reward
The Harveſt.
Pay.
The Prize.
Death.

Quies
Merces
Meſſis
Stipendium
Palma
Mors
} excipit {
Laborem.
Opus.
Sementem.
Militiam.
Curſum.
Vitam.

Peace
Plenty
Pride
Diſcord
War
Poverty
Humility
} breeds {
Plenty.
Pride.
Diſcord.
War.
Poverty.
Humility.
Peace.

Abundantia
Saturitas
Pigritia
Egeſtas
Fames
Induſtria
Ars
} comitatur {
Artem.
Abundantiam.
Saturitatem.
Pigritiam.
Egeſtatem.
Famem.
Induſtriam.

Lis odium generat. Concordia nutrit amorem.
Ira parit litem : Jurgia ſolvit amor.

A

A Bank bounds a River.   Aves faciunt nidos.
The shore breaks the Sea.   Apes struunt favos.
The brink contains a Well.   Araneæ texunt telas.
An Hedge incloses a Field.   Sciurus frangit nuces.
A Bulwark defends an Army.   Sus vorat glandes.
A Wall surrounds a City.   Talpæ fodiunt cubilia.

Vallat spina rosas, prætentant hordea spicas.
Oftrea testa tegit, cornua taurus habet.

A Soldier		a Sword.	Pileo		Pileos.
A Reaper		a Sickle.	Sutor		Calceos.
A Ditcher		a Spade.	Bibliopola		Libros.
A Taylor		a Needle.	Chirothecarius		Chirothecas.
A Cobler	buyes	an Awl.	Candelarius	vendit	Candelas.
A Barber		a Rasor.	Sutor		Ocreas.
A Weaver		a Shuttle.	Pistor		Panes.
A Dyer		a Copper.	Lanius		Carnes.
A Clothier		wooll.	Pectinarius		Pectines.
A Scholar		Books.	Pellio		Pelles.

Nauta regit navem, currus auriga gubernat.
Vertit arator humum, Plaustra bubulcus agit.

Scruta polit polio, Condensat pileo lanas.
Ligna faber fabricat, Tornio tornat ebur.

Tornio tornat mensas.   A Burler twitches knots.
Victor viet dolia.   A Shearman shears flocks.
Sartor sarcit vestes.   A Clothworker furbishes garments.
Sutor suit calceos.   A Dyer dye's cloaths.

Pensa trahit netrix, Orditur stamina textor.
Fullo lavat pannos, Mango resarcit opus.

Observ. 1. These are called Verbs Active or Transitive.
2. The emphatical parts of a sentence are the front and
rear. Hither the Verb is often transposed. Vendit pileos pileo,
Calceos sutor vendit.

Nutri

Nutrit nil ignis, Tellus animalia pascit.
 Scindit avis nubes, Flumina piscis amat.

The Gun breaks. The Gun breaks a Gate.
A Candle burns. A Candle burns a Thred.
The Ale cools. The Window cools the Ale.
The Father of a Fool grieves. A Fool grieves the Father.
The Thief hangs. The Hang-man hangs a Thief.
The Ale heats. The Fire heats the Ale.
The Wax melts. The Fire melts the Wax.
The Heart rejoyces. Success rejoyces the Heart.
Timber rots. Water rots Timber.
A King rules. A King rules the people.
The Ship sinks. The Gun sinks the Ship.
The House-keeper wakes. The Cock wakes the House-keeper.

Remember some Verbs draw after them a peculiar Case.

Genitive.	Double Accusative.
Memini.	Doceo.
Reminiscor.	Rogo.
Recordor.	Posco.
Obliviscor.	Celo.
Moneo ⎫	Induor ⎫
Accuso ⎪	Moneor ⎪
Arguo ⎬ reum crimi-	Doceor ⎬ *Passives with an*
Convinco ⎪ nis	Rogor ⎪ *Accusative.*
Damno ⎪	Poscor ⎭
Absolvo ⎭	
Misereor.	
Miseresco.	
Satago.	

Dative.

Dative.		*Ablative.*
Adulor.	Commodo, Incommodo	Careo.
Blandior.	Profum, Obfum.	Egeo.
Cedo.	Placeo, Noceo.	Indigeo.
Do.	Irafcor, Minor.	Opus eft.
Edico.	Impero, Pareo.	Vaco.
Faveo.	Dominor, Servio.	Abundo.
Gratulor.	Credo, Promitto.	Affluo.
Hæreo.	Confido, Reddo.	Impleo.
Indulgeo.	Polliceor, Solvo.	Onero.
Lenocinor.	Medeor, Nubo.	Levo.
Moderor.		Æftimo
Nuro.		
Opitulor.		Emo
Parco.		
Queror.		Liciter
Refpondeo.		
Suadeo.		Vendo
Tempero.		Potior.
Valedico.		

Vefcor, vivo, creor, nefcor, fatus, editus, ortus ; Victio, fto, confto, nitor, fungor, fruor, utor, mercem pretio.

PRAXIS. V.

TO *and* for (*the ufe of another*) *are tokens of the Dative cafe.*

Ager profert.
- Herbam ovibus.
- Semina avibus.
- Flores apibus.
- Fruges hominibus.

The fire boils
- Meat for the Cook.
- Beer for the Drawer.
- Cloaths for the Dyer.
- Medicines for the Apothecaries

Sylva nuces præbet pueris, Haftilia præbet
Sylva viris. Præbet fylva feni baculum.

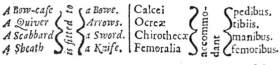

A Bow-cafe
A Quiver
A Scabbard
A Sheath
is fitted to
- a Bowe.
- Arrows.
- a Sword.
- a Knife.

Calcei
Ocreæ
Chirothecæ
Femoralia
accommodant
- pedibus.
- tibiis.
- manibus.
- femoribus.

Pifcibus

Piscibus exultant pinnæ, rota curribus ardet,
Navi vela tument, ala movetur avi.

Corn grows for the Husbandman.
Punishment is prepared for the Malefactor.
A Garland is plaited for the Conqueror.
Bands are brought for the Prisoner.

Conduntur populis leges, arx conditur urbi.
Lora crepant canibus, fræna parantur equis.

Observe after Sum *a double Dative.*

Plumæ		avibus	*Prickles*		*Roses*	Oves		Pastori.
Squamæ		piscibus	*Barbs*		*Barley*	Equi		Equisoni.
Villi	sunt integumento	canibus	*Shells*	are a (safeguard to	*Oysters*	Plantæ	sunt decori	Hortulano.
Vellera		ovibus	*Horns*		*Bulls*	Milites		Duci.
Setæ		suibus	*Nails*		*Catts*	Cives		Regi.
Capilli		capris	*Weapons*		*Men*	Discipuli		Doctori.

PRAXIS. VI.

With or By (*an Instrument*) *is a token of the Ablative case.*

A Barber shaves with a Rasor.
A Taylor sows with a Needle.
A Sawyer cuts with a Saw.
A Reaper reaps with a Sickle.

Fossor fodit ligone.
Faber dolat ascia.
Frondator lignatur securi.
Sutor suit subula.

Remo cymba movetur, aguntur lintea vento.
Bos agitur stimulo, cogitur agna pedo.

Clauditur arca serâ, signatur epistola cerâ.
Flamma alitur stipulâ, flamma domatur aquâ.

Falce seges metitur, sulcatur vomere tellus.
Cote chalybs teritur, fallitur arte labor.

Error

Error			Prudence.	Dorsum premitur onere.
Money	is	over-	Justice.	Pectus premitur curis.
Danger	come with		Fortitude.	Corpus pascitur parre.
Pleasure			Temperance.	Cor pascitur doctrinâ.

Fertur onus dorso, tolerantur pectore curæ.
Auribus ars bibitur, manditur ore cibus.

A Horse is curbed with a Bridle.	Pugna committitur jáculis.
A Ship is steered with an Helm.	Prælium cernitur gladio.
A Bull is tamed with a Yoke.	Sagittarius ferit sagittâ.
A Dog is tyed with a Chain.	Spicularius minatur spiculo.
A Lyon is restrained with Grates.	Hastaratus trajicet hastâ.
The Minde is ruled with Laws.	Tormentarius transverberat globulo.

Militat ungue leo, calamis transverberat hystrix.
Calce ferocit equus, dente minatur aper.

Observ. Time *is put in the Ablative Case.*

Vere rosæ florent, fruges æstate leguntur.
Astra die latitant, sydera nocte micant.

PRAXIS VII.

The latter of two Verbs is of the Infinitive Mood.

Piscis		pisciculos natare.	Mothers		Children to speak.
Avis	docet	aviculas volare.	Masters	teach	scholars to read.
Vermis		vermiculos repere.	Scholars		School-fellows to study.
Rana		ranunculos saltare.	Truants		School-fellows to Truant.

Nare

Nare petunt pisces, gaudent volitare volucres.
Currere geſtit equus, repere vermis avet.

A Soldier		manage a Sword.
A Clark		handle a Pen.
A Printer	knows	Print Books.
A Gardiner	to	Plant Trees.
A Lawyer		Plead Cauſes.
A Phyſitian		preſcribe Medicines.

Nauta		premere ſtivam.
Arator		gubernare clavum.
Hortulanus	neſcit	inſtruere aciem.
Imperator		agere cauſſas.
Pileo		ſuere calceos.
Sutor		cogere lanas.

Texere ſcit textor. Tinctor ſcit tingere. Netrix
Nere ſcit. Agricolæ rura domare ſciunt.

Texere vult textor. Tinctor vult tingere. Netrix
Vult nere. Agricolæ rura domare volunt.

Opportunitas		arripi.	The Sun may be overcaſt.
Hora	debet	carpi.	Vertue may be darkned.
Infamia		vitari.	Life may be extinguiſhed.
Exiſtimatio		retineri.	Fame may be ſtained.

Damna queunt redimi, cernuntur tecta renaſci.
Jacturam lucis Luna replere parat.

Creſcere barba ſolet, revireſcere cernitur arbor.
Hora redire nequit, fama redire nequit.

Aquilæ		pullos involare ſerpentes.
Feles	docent	catulos infectari mures.
Anates		ranaticulas deglutire ranas.
Vulpes		vulpeculas prædari anſeres.

The Plough-man		an Ox to bear the Yoke.
The Horſe-rider	teacheth	an Horſe to bite the Bridle.
The Miller		an Aß to turn the Mill.
The Cook		a Puppy to turn the Spit.

Pugnarum

Pugnarum gaudet memorare pericula miles.
Nauta procellarum damna referre solet.

Obſerve. *That the Infinitive of the Subſtantive Verbs draws that Caſe after it, which went before it.*

Magi ˥ dicun- ⎰ lupi Vulgus credit ⎰ magos ⎱ fieri ⎰ lupos.
Sagæ ˩ tur fieri ⎱ feles.   ⎱ ſagas ⎰   ⎱ feles.

PRAXIS VIII.

THe Prepoſition *requires a Noun in the due Caſe.*

Theſe Particles require a Noun in the Accuſative Caſe.

Infra, ſupra, ultra, citra, circa, juxta,
Erga, contra, extra, inter & intra,
Per, præter, propter, poſt, prope, pone, penes,
Ob, trans, apud, ante, ſecundum, àd, verſus, adverſus.

Frons porrigitur ⎫   ⎧ capillos.
Naſus extat   ⎬ infra ⎨ frontem.
Os aperitur   ⎪   ⎪ naſum.
Mentum prominet. ⎭   ⎩ os.

The Waters flow   ⎫   ⎧ *Earth.*
The Earth is ſtretched ⎬ *beneath* ⎨ *Clouds.*
The Clouds fleet   ⎪ *the*   ⎪ *Moon.*
The Moon is rolled ⎭   ⎩ *Sun.*

Caput nutat   ⎫   ⎧ collum.
Collum vertitur ⎬ ſupra ⎨ thoracem.
Thorax patet   ⎪   ⎪ ventrem.
Venter prominet ⎭   ⎩ pedes.

The Firmament is ſpread ⎫   ⎧ *Clouds.*
The Clouds flit   ⎬ *above* ⎨ *Trees.*
The Trees grow   ⎪ *the*   ⎪ *Earth.*
The Earth ſits   ⎭   ⎩ *Waters.*

Supra tellurem Solis clementia fulget,
Infra tellurem Luna gubernat equos.

The

The Shore rises			Sea.	Sagitta volat			Metam.
The Bank rises	}	beyond the	River.	Equus nititur	}	ultra	Calcem.
A Hedge is planted			Ditch.	Discipulus excurrit			Lectionem.
A Valley sinks			Hell.	Fama durat			Vitam.

The Shore rises			Sea.	Sagitta cadit			Metam.
The Bank rises	}	behither the	River.	Equuleus deficit	}	citra	Calcem.
A Ditch is dug			Hedge.	Cessator languet			Pensum.
A Valley sinks			Hill.	Pigritia fugit			Victoriam.

Subsistit pondus citra mare corporis, ultra
Oceani fines pectoris ala volat.

A Wall is built			A City.
A Bulwark is raised	}	about	An Army.
Hurdles are placed			A Sheepfold.
The Guard goes			The King.

Milites excubant			Praetorium.
Vallum ducitur	}	citra	Milites.
Fossa secatur			Vallum.
Equitatus excubat			Fossam.

The Sheep graze			Bank.
The Shepherd sits	}	nigh the	Sheep.
The Dog crouches			Shepherd.
The Staff lies			Dog.

Scholaris stat			Abacum.
Charta explicatur	}	juxta	Scholarem.
Cornugraphium ponitur			Chartam.
Regula jacet			Cornugraphium.

Oceanus circa tellurem porrigit undas.
Oceani juxta littus arena jacet.

Observance			A Master.	Timor			Deum.
Mildneß	}	is required towards	A Servant.	Charitas	}	exercetur erga	Homines.
Severity			A Truant.	Dilectio			Fratres.
Kindneß			A School-fellow.	Pietas			Parentes.

C

A Captain		A Captain.		Eques		Equitem.
A Soldier	fights against	A Soldier.		Pedes	ruit contra	Peditem.
A General		A General.		Nauta		Nautam.
An Army		An Army.		Navis		Navem.

Erga tutorem pupillus honore probatur,
Erga pupillum tutor amore placet.

Contra pisciculos rostrum larus exerit : Ungues
Contra perdicem dirigit accipiter.

Adversus cervos catulorum militat agmen,
Adversus lepores vertragus arma gerit.

A Bird		Cage flies.
A Scholar	without the	School skips.
A Sheep		Fold strays.
A Fish		Water dies.

Gladius		Vaginam terret.
Pecunia	extra	Crumenam follicitat.
Nudeus		Putamen pascit.
Medulla		Os nutrit.

The Brain quivers		Scull.
The Heart pants	within the	Brest.
The Blood flows		Veins.
The Marrow swells		Bones.

Urina continetur		Vesicam.
Stercus comprimitur	intra	Viscera.
Saliva spumat		Fauces.
Lac surgit		Mammas.

Rugitus intra clathrorum septa leones
Dant : Intra caveæ texta queruntur aves.

Extra clathrorum prædantur septa leones :
Cœlum extra caveæ vimina scindit avis.

The

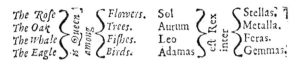

The Rose ⎫ ⎧ Flowers.   Sol ⎫ ⎧ Stellas.
The Oak ⎬ among ⎨ Trees.   Aurum ⎬ est Rex inter ⎨ Metalla.
The Whale ⎨ the Queen ⎬ Fishes.   Leo ⎨ ⎬ Feras.
The Eagle ⎭ ⎩ Birds.   Adamas ⎭ ⎩ Gemmas.

Inter aquas Balæna petit Regina vocari.
Inter aves Aquilæ regna tenere petunt.

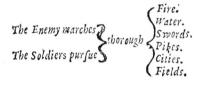

The Enemy marches ⎫ thorough ⎧ Fire.
                   ⎬   ⎨ Water.
                   ⎪   ⎪ Swords.
The Soldiers pursue ⎭   ⎨ Pikes.
                              ⎪ Cities.
                              ⎩ Fields.

Lepus fugit   ⎫ ⎧ Montes.
                 ⎪ ⎨ Valles.
                 ⎪ ⎪ Silvas.
                 ⎬ per ⎨ Amnes.
Catuli sequuntur ⎭ ⎪ Sæpem.
                   ⎩ Fossam.

Per Sola mors homines sternit : Mors per mare Pisces
Solvit : Per cœlum mors populatur aves.

Repere vermis avet per humum : Volitare per auras
Gaudet avis : Piscis per mare nare petit.

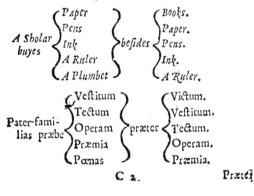

A Sholar ⎧ Paper   ⎫ besides ⎧ Books.
buyes   ⎪ Pens   ⎪   ⎨ Paper.
         ⎨ Ink   ⎬   ⎨ Pens.
         ⎪ A Ruler ⎪   ⎪ Ink.
         ⎩ A Plumbet ⎭   ⎩ A Ruler.

Pater-fami- ⎧ Vestitum ⎫ præter ⎧ Victum.
lias præbe ⎪ Tectum   ⎪   ⎨ Vestitum.
            ⎨ Operam   ⎬   ⎨ Tectum.
            ⎪ Præmia   ⎪   ⎪ Operam.
            ⎩ Pœnas   ⎭   ⎩ Præmia.

Præter balænam Delphin graſſatur in undis.
Præter vulturium milvius urget aves.

Abſinthium hauritur			Lumbricos.
Glycyrrhiza manducatur	} propter {		Tuſſim.
Carduus bibitur			Febrem.
Sulphur inungitur			Scabiem.

Laus impertitur			Diligentiam.
Pudor incutitur	} ob {		Negligentiam.
Præmium aſſignatur			Modeſtiam.
Supplicium infertur			Petulantiam.

Becauſe of

The Trumpet ſounds			Judge.
The Bell rings	} before {		Aſſembly.
The Alarum is heard	the		Battle.
The Token is given			Race.

Lucifer micat			Diem.
Heſperus oritur	} ante {		Noctem.
Turdi diſcedunt			Ver.
Hirundines adveniunt			Æſtatem.

Reſt			Labor.
A Reward	} is obtained {		Work.
Harveſt	after		Seed-time.
Pay			Warfare.
The Prize			The Race.

Pueritia			Infantiam.
Adoleſcentia			Pueritiam.
Juventus	} ſequitur poſt {		Adoleſcentiam.
Senectus			Juventutem.
Mors			Senectutem.

Poſt curſum Solis venit Heſperus ante tenebras.
Poſt tenebras oritur Lucifer ante Diem.

The Soldiers		Captain.	Princeps		Regem.
The Children	} go behind the {	Father.	Judex	} incedit pone {	Principem.
The Servants		Maſter.	Eques		Judicem.
The Maids		Miſtreß.	Plebs		Equitem.

Panis

Panis	} habetur penes {	Piftorem.	Linum	} habetur penes {	Linteonem.
Caro		Lanium.	Lana		Paftorem.
Vinum		Cauponem.	Corium		Sutorem.
Frumentum		Agricolam	Materia		Fabrum.

Pons ducitur trans foffam. Portitor vehit trans amnem,

Clientes	} tendunt verfus {	Patronum.
Rei	veniunt ad	Iudicem.
Medici	manent apud	Ægrum.
Equi		Veterinarium.

Marriners	} *bend towards* {	*Ship.*
Soldiers	*come to*	*Army.*
Pleaders	*abide at* *the*	*Town-houfe.*
Scholars		*School.*

Note, that Verfus *is put after its* Accufative, as, Clientes tendunt patronum verfus.

Proceres incedunt	} fecundum {	Dignitatem.
Difcipuli fedent		Doctrinam.
Milites laudantur		Virtutem.
Mercatores æftimantur		Divitias.

Death is expected	} *accord-ing to* {	*Nature.*
Crimes are punifhed		*Law.*
Wealth is fined		*Cuftom.*
Mercy is exercifed		*Will.*

Thefe Particles require a Noun in the Ablative Cafe.

Abs, ex, cum, coram, præ, pro, fine, de , tenus, abfque.

Helluo dif-currit	} {	à tabernâ	} ad {	tabernam.
		à cauponâ		cauponam.
		à popinâ		popinam.
		à lupanari		lupanar.

The

The Begger wanders from { place / chimney / door / street } to { place. / chimney. / door. / street. }

A ponto veniunt amnes. Ros stillat ab auris,
Lux à nocte subit. Grana vigent ab humo.

Ad pontum remeant amnes, Vapor halat ad auras.
Nox redit ad lucem. Grana ruunt ad humum.

Flores / Nuces / Pisces / Grana } colliguntur ex { Hortis. / Sylvis. / Amnibus. / Agris.

Wine / Oyl / Milk / Honey } is squeezed out of { Grapes. / Olives. / Dugs. / Honey-combs.

Agnus eripitur ex ore lupi.
Lepus effugit é rictu canis.

Columba evolat é rostro acci-
(pitris.
Anguilla elabitur è manu pis-
(catoris.

Ex Zephyro tepor aspirat, Delabitur humor
Ex Austro, Densant ex Aquilone nives.

Puer / Adolescens / Vir / Senex / Anus / Veteranus } fit ex { Infante. / Puero. / Adolescente. / Viro. / Puellâ. / Tirone.

Cervus / Caper / Ovis / Pullus / Canis / Aper } fit ex { Hinulo. / Hædo. / Agno. / Ovo. / Catulo. / Verre.

Arbor / Malus / Pyrus / Prunus / Cerasus / Vitis } fit ex { Fructu. / Malo. / Pyro, / Pruno. / Ceraso. / Uvâ.

Ex ovo fit avis, Quercûs ex glande feruntur.
Ex vitulo fit bos, Ex catulo Leo fit.

Labor

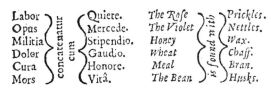

Labor		Quiete.	The Rose		Prickles.
Opus		Mercede.	The Violet		Nettles.
Militia	concatenatur cum	Stipendio.	Honey	is found with	Wax.
Dolor		Gaudio.	Wheat		Chaff.
Cura		Honore.	Meal		Bran.
Mors		Vitâ.	The Bean		Husks.

Mufta fluunt cum fæce. Trapetis manat olivum
Cum fracibus. Ponti cum fale fpumat aqua.

Cum maculis Sol confpicitur. Cum fordibus aurum
Nafcitur. Eft nævo cum probitate locus.

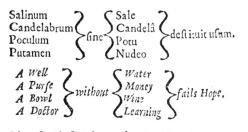

Salinum		Sale	
Candelabrum	fine	Candelâ	deftituit ufum.
Poculum		Potu	
Putamen		Nudeo	

A Well		Water	
A Purfe	without	Money	fails Hope.
A Bowl		Wine	
A Doctor		Learning	

Mens fine doctrinâ, mundus fine fole videtur,
Abfque jugo cãnis eft, abfque pudore puer.

Proceres apparent coram rege. Reus fiftitur coram judice.

Æs præ ferro		Oculi ardent		Irâ.
Argentum præ ære	eligitur.	Genæ rubent	præ	Pudore.
Aurum præ argento		Cor falit		Gaudio.
Virtus præ auro		Manus tremunt		Timore.

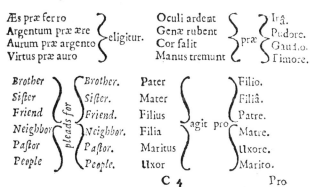

Brother		Brother.	Pater		Filio.
Sifter		Sifter.	Mater		Filiâ.
Friend	pleads for	Friend.	Filius	agit pro	Patre.
Neighbor		Neighbor.	Filia		Matre.
Paftor		Paftor.	Maritus		Uxore.
People		People.	Uxor		Marito.

C 4

Pro

Pro grege pervigilat paſtor. Pro milite curas
Dux patitur, Miles pro duce bella gerit.

The Phyſitian			Diſeaſes.	Arator			tauris.
The Soldier	*diſcurris*	*concernit*	Battles.	Paſtor	*differit de*		ovibus.
The Lawyer			Laws.	Venator			nibus.
The Merchant			Ships.	Diſcipulus			bris.

Chirothecæ		cubito		Foſſorm	genuum
	explicantur		tenus		adeſt tenus,
Ocreæ		pube		Piſcator	aurium

Obſerve tenus *is put after the Caſe, and is joyn'd to the
Genitive of Plurals in the third declenſion.*

Theſe ſerve to Accuſative and Ablative, Sub, ſubter, ſuper
in, clam.

In *and* ſub *after Verbs of motion require an Accuſative Caſe
otherwiſe an Ablative.*

Pecus			umbras.	A Ship			a Harbor.
Canis	*abditur ſub*		menſam.	A Hare	*flies under*		a Heath.
Felis			lectum.	A Stag			a Thicket.
Vermis			terram.	A Soldier			a Caſtle.

Navis			portu.	Fruits			Trees.
Lepus	*latet ſub*		ericeto.	Acorns	*lye under*		an Oak.
Cervus			fruticeto.	Nuts			an Hazel.
Miles			turri.	Dates			a Palm.

		aſſembles into	the Church.
The people			the Town-houſe.
		ſits in	the Court.
			a Ship.

Diſcipuli

$$\text{Discipuli} \begin{cases} \text{conveniunt in} \begin{cases} \text{Auditorium.} \\ \text{Scholam.} \\ \text{Aulam.} \\ \text{Cubiculum.} \end{cases} \\ \\ \text{manent in} \begin{cases} \text{Auditorio.} \\ \text{Scholâ.} \\ \text{Aulâ.} \\ \text{Cubiculo.} \end{cases} \end{cases}$$

Sub terram repunt vermes, sub flumina Pisces
  Merguntur, stagni sub vada rana salit.

Sunt sub aquis ranæ, sunt sub torrente Lapilli.
  Sub terra rostro talpa cubile fodit.

In mare flumen abit, flammæ nituntur in auras.
  Ros cadit in terras, tendit in astra vapor.

In sylvis fera regnat, aves spatiantur in auris.
  Piscis in undarum gurgite radit iter.

*Super upon with either Accusative or Ablative, about with
an Ablative.*

$$\text{Vacca} \atop \text{Equus} \atop \text{Nauta} \atop \text{Miles} \quad \text{cubat super} \begin{cases} \text{frondibus.} \\ \text{stramine.} \\ \text{tabulis.} \\ \text{gramine.} \end{cases} \qquad \text{Glacies} \atop \text{Nix} \atop \text{Pluvia} \atop \text{Ærumna} \quad \text{germinatur super} \begin{cases} \text{glaciem.} \\ \text{nivem.} \\ \text{pluviam.} \\ \text{ærumnam.} \end{cases}$$

Pater rogat super filio, Filius rogat super patre.
  Discipulus lusitat clam magistro. Reus fugit clam custode.

More anciently it was joyned to an Accusative; as also
clanculum.

*The use of the Latine does often put the Preposition to the
Verb which is compounded with it.*

Rota circumvertitur axem.   Amnis præterfluit urbem.
Mare circumlabitur orbem.   Navis prætervehit arcem.
Littus circumsedet aquor.   Volucris prætervolat agros.
Sol circumvolvitur annum.   Piscis præternatat algas.

Puer per legit lectionem.   Puer relegit lectionem.
Puer perscribit dictamen.   Puer rescribit dictamen.
Autor peragit opus.   Tinctor recoquit pannum.
Discipulus percurrit pensum.   Textor retexit telam.

Ambit lympha solum.   Tellus amplectitur undam.

Verbs compounded with ab, ex, de, pro, *govern ordinarily an Ablative Case.*

Usually a Dative Case follows Verbs compounded with sub, super, ad, (cum) con, præ, post, ob, in, inter, & ante.

Rex superponit coronam capiti.
Victor supponit caput coronæ.
Hospes apponit cibum hospiti.
Dapifer imponit cibum mensæ.
Discipulus interponit lusum studiis.
Athleta opponit artem viribus.

Philosophus
{ componit aurum virtutibus.
{ anteponit } virtutes auro.
{ præponit }
{ postponit aurum virtutibus.

Observe in composition how the end of the Preposition compounding, or the first Vowel of the Verb compounded changes.

Ad	Sub	Ob
Accumbo.	Succumbo.	Occumbo.
Affundo.	Suffundo.	Offundo.
Aggero.	Suggero.	Oggero.
Appono.	Suppono.	Oppono.

In *before* b, p, *and* m, *is* im : *before* r *and* l *takes the same letter.* Con *before Vowels, and* h *leaves out* n : *before* b, p. *and* m *is* com ; *before* r *and* l *takes the same letter.* Ex *is* e *before* b, d, g, l, m, n, r, j, *and* v, *and* epoto *onely.* *Although in Ancient and in Country words, it abides before those Letters.*

So for Verbs, some turn the first a *into* e, *others turn the first* a, æ, *or* e, *into* i, *three into* u : Calco, Salto, Quatio ; *three omit* a Causo, Claudo, Lavo.

Em-

Emptor
tranſit ab { Officinâ
Urbe
Emporio
Regione } ad { Officinam.
Urbem.
Emporium.
Regionem.

Textor
Tornio
Nauclerus
Venditor } ſedet ad { Jugum.
Tornum.
Clavum.
Tabernam.

Pannificus
Lanius
Piſtor
Bibliopola } tendit { Netorem
Paſtorem
Molitorem
Typographum } verſus.

Merces
Naulum
Minerval
Soſtrum } debetur ob { Opus.
Vecturam.
Inſtitutionem.
Medelam.

Hoſpes
Vector
Conviva
Amicus } eſt apud { Hoſpitem.
Navem.
Menſam.
Amicum.

Servus
Pupillus
Filius
Merx } eſt penes { Dominum.
Tutorem.
Patrem.
Mercatorem.

Inſtrumentum
Falx
Tribula
Cribum } eſt propter { Opificem.
Meſſorem.
Tritorem.
Piſtorem.

Radius
Subula
Acus
Serra } tranſit per { Telam.
Corium.
Pannum.
Lignum.

Artifex
Tibicen
Poeta
Orator } certat ad-verſus { Artificem.
Tibicinem.
Poetam.
Oratorem.

Sartor
Scriba
Pharmacopola
Fiſſor } poſcit { Filum
Atramentum
Mortarium
Cuneum } præter { Acum.
Pennam.
Piſtillum.
Malleum.

Olitor

Olitor
Vinitor
Mellarius
Discipulus
} oblectatur inter {
Olera.
Uvas.
Alvearia.
Libros.

Molendinum ponitur
Salinæ fodiuntur
Diversorium patet
Torcular struitur
} juxta {
Fluvium.
Mare.
Viam.
Vineam.

Gladius
Culter
Arcus
Sagitta
} nitet extra
cohibetur inter {
Vaginam.
Thecam.
Corytum.
Pharetram.

Opus fit ab opifice.
Mensa tornatur à tornione.
Dolium vietur à vietore.
Vestis farcitur à sartore.
Calceus suitur à sutore.

Opus fit ex materiâ.
Mensa tornatur ex ligno.
Panis subigitur ex farinâ.
Pannus texitur ex lanâ.
Calceus suitur ex corio.

Opifex
Faber
Sartor
Sutor
Textor
} certat cum {
Opifice.
Fabro.
Sartore.
Sutore.
Textore.

Artifex
Coquus
Sartor
Nauclerus
} laudatur præ {
Opifice.
Lixâ.
Veteramentario.
Cerdone.
Remige.

Opifex
Faber
Sartor
Sutor
Textor
} cessat sine {
Instrumento.
Regulâ.
Acu.
Subulâ.
Radio.

Opifex
Arator
Venator
Miles
Discipulus
} loquitur de {
Opere.
Bobus.
Canibus.
Præliis.
Libris.

Miles pugnat
Remex nititur
Discipulus studet
Servus laborat
Ancilla laborat
} coram {
Duce.
Hortatore.
Magistro.
Domino.
Dominâ.

Stipendium
Naulum
Sostrum
Comistrum
Merces
} solvitur pro {
Militiâ.
Vecturâ.
Medelâ.
Bajulatione.
Opere.

Mercator

Mercator

quærit subsidia contra { solicitudines. / paupertatem.

relinquit uxorem cis { fluvios / maria } citra { labores. / pericula.

proficiscitur à patriâ { exponitur sub { dium. / aquas.
solvit à portu

sequitur pone { præterem / præsidium } cubat sub { dio / aquis } supe { paleâ / pellibus (a)

(a) { cum { nautis / mercatoribus } absque { stragulis. / culcitâ.

fertur adversus { socios. / hostes.

vehitur per { fluvios / maria } præter { syrtes / scopulos } inter { prædones / procellas (b)

(b) { prope { naufragium / captivitatem } circum { montes / valles (c)

(c) { ltra { terras / stellas } Barbaros / Hospites } versus.

currit trans { fluvios / maria } jactature { terrâ / nave } in { navem. / terram.

patitur { frigora / calores } ante { hyemem / æstatem } aspergitur { genuum / mento } tenus.

moratur extra { domum / patriam } intra { navem / hospitium } apud { Barbaros / Hospites (d)

(d) { procul { uxore. / liberis.

Mercator

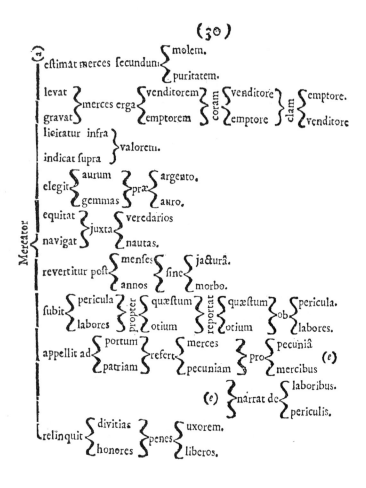

estimat merces secundum { molem. / puritatem.

levat } merces erga { venditorem } coram { venditore } clam { emptore. / venditore }
gravat } { emptorem } { emptore }

licitatur infra } valorem.
indicat supra }

elegit { aurum } præ { argento. / auro. }
{ gemmas }

equitat } juxta { veredarios / nautas. }
navigat }

revertitur post { menses / annos } sine { jacturâ. / morbo. }

subit { pericula } propter { quæstum } reportat { quæstum } ob { pericula. / labores. }
{ labores } { otium } { otium }

appellit ad { portum } refert { merces } pro { pecuniâ / mercibus } (e)
{ patriam } { pecuniam }

(e) } narrat de { laboribus. / periculis. }

relinquit { divitias } penes { uxorem. / liberos. }
{ honores }

Meteator

PRAXIS.

PRAXIS IX.

Substantive and Adjective agree in Gender, Case, and Number.

Nouns receive Gender first from their signification of Male or Female, as

Equus, Lupus, Sponsus, Dominus, *Masculine*
a &
Agnus, Cervus, Filius, Servus. *Feminine.*

or neither of the two, as Saxum, Metallum, Lignum, Mare,

Patri filius hæret, Adhæret filia matri.
Servus herum sequitur. Serva ministrat heræ.

Some being common in signification are of both Genders.

Augur,	Vates,	Dux,	Hostis,
Antistes,	Civis,	Comes,	Judex,
Sacerdos,	Municeps,	Miles,	Vindex,
Autor,	Parens,	Conjux,	Sus.
Custos,	Patruelis,	Infans,	Bos.
Conviva,	Affinis,	Hæres,	Canis.

Or secondly, They receive Gender from their declension (considering the termination) by these Nine Rules.

a *Plural is Neuter* Caput ita Labrum a

i *Masculine* Oculus i

æ *Feminine* Gena æ

{ Alvus, vannus, humus, domus,
Names of Trees fagus, ulmus,
Some Greek words, as Papyrus, &c. } *are Feminine.*

es { *not increasing is Feminine* Auris es[a].
from one Syllable is Feminine Vox ces[b].
increasing long is Feminine Cervix ices[c].
short is Masculine Vertex ices[d].

ûs *Masculine* Vultus ûs.
es *Feminine* Facies ês.

a Er

[a] Er ceu venter, is orbis, fafcis, Pifcis & unguis,
Callis, caulis, follis, collis, menfis, & enfis,
Vermis, funis, panis, penis, crinis, & ignis,
Torris, vectis, fentis, poftis, fuftis, & axis.

One Syllables are Feminine, except
[b] Sal, Sol, mos, flos, ros, ren, fplen, dens, pes fimul as, bes,
Seps, grips, mons, pons, fons, grex, glis fimul exiguus müs,
En lichen, o Sermo, in io verbalia tolle,
Mafcula in er, or & os craterque, laborque, labofque.

Danto genus muliebre fuperbiffyllaba do, go,
Drando, teges, feges, arbor, hyems, compes, pecudefque,
Ys clamys, is pyxis, nec non as græcula lampas,
Caffis, item cufpis, carex, forfexque filixque,
Appendix & coxendix & lauta fupellex.

The doubtful abound } *in Gender.*
The epicæne are deficient }

Adjectives are of the firft and fecond Declenfion in us *and* r,
with three terminations Verus a um, Afper a um. *The Maf-
culine and Neuter are of the firft, the Feminine is of the fecond Declenfion, or of the third Declenfion in* is, *with two
terminations, as* Gravis e; *others in the Nominative fingular,
are but of one termination in* x velox, us vetus, rs folers, ns
fapiens, es dives, ar par. *Some in* er pauper, *others in* er *have
three terminations* celer is e.

	Singulariter		Pluraliter
N. Verus, a, um.		N. Veri, æ, a,	
G. Veri, æ.		G. Verorum, arum,	
Acc. Verum, am.		Acc. Veros, as.	
D. Vero, æ.		D. } Veris.	
Abl. Vero, â.		Abl. }	

	Singulariter		Pluraliter
N. Gravis, e.		N. Graves, ia.	
G. Gravis.		G. Gravium.	
Acc. Gravem.		Acc. Graves.	
D. } Gravi.		D. } Gravibus.	
Abl. }		Abl. }	

[a] Duo, æ, o; fo D. & Abl. obus, abus, ambo likewife.
[b] Adjectives of one termination make their D. Sing. in i. Abl. in e

The

The practice of the Gender may be by prefixing Hic, hæc, hoc.

Hic liber eft novus.	*This Hearth is cold.*
Hæc charta eft bibula.	*This School is empty.*
Hoc dictamen eft mendofum.	*This Bench is naked.*
Hæc veftis eft pulverulenta.	*This Form is idle.*
Hæc lex eft rigida.	*This Beam is ftrong.*
Hæc lectio eft longa.	*This Weather is hot.*
Hic canon eft rectus.	*This Wall is fullied.*
Hic gradus eft altus.	*This Play is unfeafonable.*
Hæc acies eft obtufa.	*This Face is foul.*

Sometimes the Verb Subftantive is omitted, as, Ars longa, Vita brevis. Magifter mitis, Puer fedulus, Condifcipuli humani, Methodus facilis, Tempus charum, Nihil adverfum, Nemo invidus.

Vinum		calidum.	Honey		*fweet.*
Aqua	eft	frigida.	*Wormwood*	is	*bitter.*
Crocus		puniceus.	*The Rofe*		*tender.*
Lac		candidum.	*The Thorn*		*rough.*

Vinum generofum inebriat.	*Sweet Honey gluts.*
Aqua tenuis refrigerat.	*Bitter Wormwood cures.*
Lilium pulchrum delectat.	*The tender Rofe pricks.*
Pomum mire pafcit.	*The rough Thorn fences.*

Gravitas fentinæ fætidæ	
Facies carceris tenebrofi	offendit.
Stridor ferræ afperæ	
Sapor abfinthii amari	

	Sent of a fweet Perfume		
The	*Sight of a fair Picture*	*delights.*	
	Melody of a tunable Lute		
	Tafte of a generous Wine		

Equifo		equum nitidum.	
Paftor	cupit	oves pingues.	
Vinitor		vineam apricam.	
Hortulanus		hortum irriguum.	

	Horfe		*rank Paftures.*
The	*Sheep*	*loves*	*the tender Herb.*
	Vineyard		*warm Hills.*
	Garden		*frefh Moifture.*

D

Seges

Seges luxuriat agricolæ impigro.
Carmina fluunt poetæ ingeniofo.
Oratio torret oratori diferto.
Doctrina procedit difcipulo ftudiofo.

Clients fwarm to a skilful Lawyer.
The Threfhold is worn to a faithful Phyficiax.
Glory lafts to an uncorrupt Judge.
Work abounds to an accute Artift.

Animus {
  Inflatur honoribus immodicis.
  Diftrahitur opibus nimiis.
  Gravatur doloribus ingentibus.
  Erigitur alloquiis mitibus.
  Alitur confiliis falubribus.
}

The Stomack is {
  Pampered with delicate Junckets.
  Fed with folid Meats.
  Relieved with bitter Potions.
  Oppreft with various Difhes.
  Cheared with hot Liquors.
}

The foft Brain quivers within the hard Scull.
The quick Heart pants within the broad Breft.
The red Blood flows within the blew Veins.
The moyft Marrow fwells within the hollow Bones.

Margaritæ candidæ latent intra mare profundum.
Venæ metalliferæ Serpunt intra terram opacam.
Feræ pervigiles fedent intra fylvas denfas.
Ranæ importunæ coaxant intra paludes limofas.

Firmamentum ftellatum		Regionem aeriam.
Regio aeria	explica-	Globum terreftrem.
Equitatus levis	tur extra	Propugnaculum firmum
Propugnaculum firmum		Peditatum tutum.

A {
  deep Cellar,
  fpacious Hall,
  handfome Chamber,
  high Garret,
} *lies be- neath* {
  a fpacious Hall.
  a handfome Chamber.
  a high Garret.
  a firm Roof.
}

Nafus fagax		Frontem patentem.
Os vocale	eft infra	Nafum fagacem.
Mentum pendulum		Os vocale.
Collum teres		Mentum pendulum.

A

A {
Merchant sails
Soldier charges
Huntsman rushes
Scholar passes
} through {
vast Seas.
sharp Swords.
thick Woods.
many difficulties.
}

A Truant blames {
a difficult English,
a naughty Pen,
clotty Ink,
sinking Paper,
} besides {
a long Lesson.
a difficult English,
a naughty Pen.
clotty Ink.
}

Labor durus
Opus difficile
Militia aspera
Prælium acre·
Cursus impiger
} absolvitur ante {
quietem mollem.
mercedem justam.
stipendium charum.
victoriam dulcem.
palmam illustrem.
}

Joyful Peace
Clear Light
The welcome Harvest
Heavy disgrace
Bitter weeping
} follows after {
sad War.
the dark Night.
the wet Seed-time.
filthy Pleasure.
sweet Laughter.
}

The {
starry Arches
fleeting Clouds
mountany Woods
wide Plains
} are raised above the {
fleeting Clouds.
mountainy Woods.
wide Plains.
deep Waters.
}

Garments
Meats
Houses
Medicines
} are provided against {
quivering cold.
biting hunger.
vehement storms.
various diseases.
}

The {
Barley
Wheat
Peach
Rose
} grows with {
sharp Barbs.
the light Chaff.
soft Down.
rough Prickles.
}

A Ship reels
A Horse flings
The Thoughts wander
The Mind swells
} without {
a just ballast.
a stiff snaffle.
honest employments.
the Divine Law.
}

Spices
Furrs
} are brought from {
hot
cold
} climes.

Sands are scattered in dry places.
Herbs are generated in wet Fenns.

ÆT as est fugitiva, dies alata recedit,
    Firma juventa perit, tardà senecta subit.
Aurea Sol rutilæ permittit fræna diei,
    Obscuræ noctis Luna flagellat equos.
Crastina lux noctem pellit. Nox altera lucem
    Trudit, iners tempus mobilis hora rapit.
Luna vetus renovare parat dispendia lucis
    Plena novam lucem perdere Luna parat.
Post hyemem gelidam tepidum ver incipit. Almum
    Post ver æstivo terra vapore calet.
Sub tutas umbras pecus omne recumbit, ab umbris
    Amnes ad tristes cogitur omne pecus.
Autumnus calidam post messem poma ministrat,
    Post madidum autumnum bruma recurrit iners.
Villicus hyberni contra vim frigoris acrem
    Arida sublimi de strue ligna trahit.
Ingens ventosis excitur follibus ignis,
    Tota domus clarum desidet ante focum :
Ad præsepe boves fræno jejunia solvunt,
    Aspergit durum cana pruina solum.
Subducit naves siccas in littora tuta
    Nauta piger : Tumidi tollitur ira freti.
Orbe brevi pronum Sol præceps conficit annum
    Sol redit : Orbe pari proximus annus abit.
Infanti tenero veniunt discrimina multa
    Incauto iuveni crimina multa placent,
Multa viro firmo curarum copia surgit :
    Invalido morbi dant mala multa seni.
Sola manet virtus ; Virtus sublimior astris
    Altior è terris regna superna petit.

Tutrices

TVtrices prohibent immitia frigora vestes,
  Vela verecundus quærit honesta pudor.
Pilea lata premunt umbroso margine frontem,
  Nudus conspicui cernitur ovis honos.
Lactea colla decent collaria pura, Lacertis
  Dant niveis manicæ vincula pura pares.
Virginibus teneris decus ist armilla. Tyrannis
  Gemmatum circum colla monile sedet.
Compar multiforem thoracem fibula nectit
  Hamatas caligas excipit ansa tenax.
Incurvus patulis immittitur uncus ocellis :
  Ferratas squamas aura subire nequit,
Cingula dividuas renuunt committere braccas,
  Zonarum cinctus integra vestis amat.
Discrimen femorum geminum femoralia produnt,
  Tibia de proprio nomine tegmen habet.
Calceus aptatur pedibus de pelle bovina,
  Vaginam manibus pellis ovina parat.

Remember

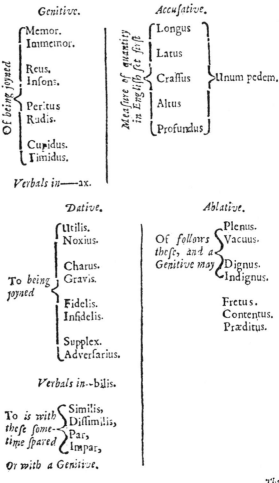

Remember some Adjectives draw after them a Case.

Genitive.

Of being joyned
{
Memor.
Immemor.

Reus.
Infons.

Peritus.
Rudis.

Cupidus.
Timidus.
}

Verbals in——ax.

Accusative.

Measure of quantity in English set first
{
Longus

Latus

Craffus

Altus

Profundus
}
Unum pedem.

Dative.

To being joyned
{
Utilis.
Noxius.

Charus.
Gravis.

Fidelis.
Infidelis.

Supplex.
Adverfarius.
}

Verbals in--bilis.

To *is with* thefe fome--time fpared
{
Similis,
Diffimilis,
Par,
Impar,
}

Or with a Genitive.

Ablative.

Of *follows* thefe, *and a* Genitive *may*
{
Plenus.
Vacuus.

Dignus.
Indignus.
}

Fretus.
Contentus.
Præditus.

The

The *whole described by its part, with the property, puts it in the Ablative.*

Pavo eſt ales gemmatâ caudâ.
Palumbes eſt avis annulato collo.
Veſpertilio eſt animal membranaceis alis.
Papilio eſt inſectum picto corpore.
Talpa eſt beſtiola craſſis oculis.
Camelus eſt jumentum gibboſo dorſo.

PRAXIS X.

THen *after a* Comparative *is a token of the Ablative Caſe.*
The *Adjective in the* Poſitive *degree is given with* Number.
The Comparative *turns the Plural* i *into* ior.
The Superlative *es* iſſimus.

er *Poſitive* errimus.
lis *in three*,

Facilis ⎫
Humilis ⎬llimus.
Similis ⎭

Bonus, Melior, Optimus.   Magnus, Major, Maximus.
Malus, Pejor, Peſſimus.   Parvus, Minor, Minimus.

Multus, a, um.
plus.
Plurimus.

wiſdom					
Luxury	⎫	⎧*pretiouſer*	⎫	⎧*a Jewel.*	
Diſgrace	⎬ *is*	⎨*crueller*	⎬*then*	⎨*War.*	
Induſtry	⎭	⎩*grievouſer*	⎭	⎩*Poverty.*	
		richer		*Sloth.*	

Gemma			
Bellum	⎫	⎧Vilior Sapientiâ.	
Paupertas	⎬ eſt	⎨Mitius Luxuriâ.	
Pigritia	⎭	⎩Levior Infamiâ.	
		Pauperior Induſtriâ.	

D 4   Luna

$$
\left.\begin{array}{l}
\text{Luna} \\
\text{Amnis} \\
\text{Frutex} \\
\text{Nox}
\end{array}\right\} \text{est} \left\{\begin{array}{l}
\text{obſcurior Sole.} \\
\text{anguſtior mari.} \\
\text{humilior arbore.} \\
\text{triſtior die.}
\end{array}\right.
$$

$$
\left.\begin{array}{l}
\textit{The Sun} \\
\textit{The Sea} \\
\textit{A Tree} \\
\textit{The day}
\end{array}\right\} \textit{is} \left\{\begin{array}{l}
\textit{brighter} \\
\textit{wider} \\
\textit{higher} \\
\textit{pleaſanter}
\end{array}\right\} \textit{then} \left\{\begin{array}{l}
\textit{the Moon.} \\
\textit{a River.} \\
\textit{a Shrub.} \\
\textit{The Night.}
\end{array}\right.
$$

$$
\left.\begin{array}{l}
\text{Operarius} \\
\text{Foſſor} \\
\text{Corbulo} \\
\text{Bajulus} \\
\text{Bubulcus} \\
\text{Remex}
\end{array}\right\} \text{est illibe-} \atop \text{ralior} \left\{\begin{array}{l}
\text{opifice.} \\
\text{hortulano.} \\
\text{cœmentario.} \\
\text{ferrario.} \\
\text{agricolâ.} \\
\text{nauclero.}
\end{array}\right.
$$

$$
\left.\begin{array}{l}
\textit{An Artiſt} \\
\textit{A Gardiner} \\
\textit{A Bricklayer} \\
\textit{A Smith} \\
\textit{A Husbandman} \\
\textit{A Pilot}
\end{array}\right\} \textit{is worthier} \atop \textit{then} \left\{\begin{array}{l}
\textit{a Laborer.} \\
\textit{a Ditcher.} \\
\textit{an Hodman.} \\
\textit{a Porter.} \\
\textit{a Carter.} \\
\textit{a Rower.}
\end{array}\right.
$$

$$
\left.\begin{array}{l}
\textit{By} \\
\textit{Then}
\end{array}\right\} \textit{notes the} \left\{\begin{array}{l}
\textit{meaſure.} \\
\textit{term.}
\end{array}\right.
$$
Quanto opperarius eſt illibe-
ralior opifice,
Tanto corbulo eſt indignior
cœmentario.

By how much an Artiſt is more creditable then a Laborer,
By ſo much a Bricklayer is worthier then a Hodman.

$$
\left.\begin{array}{l}
\text{Rex} \\
\text{Princeps} \\
\text{Dux} \\
\text{Comes} \\
\text{Senator} \\
\text{Eques}
\end{array}\right\} \text{appellatur} \left\{\begin{array}{l}
\text{ſereniſſimus.} \\
\text{celſiſſimus.} \\
\text{excellentiſſimus.} \\
\text{honoratiſſimus.} \\
\text{ſapientiſſimus.} \\
\text{illuſtriſſimus.}
\end{array}\right.
$$

An Orator		eloquent.
A Poet		ingenious.
A Lawyer	is stiled most	practised.
A Physitian		faithful.
A Master		vigilant.
A Scholar		studious.

Vinum generosissimum accessit.   The sweetest Honey gluts.
Pomum mitissimum putrescit.   The bitterest Wormwood cures.
Rosa suavissima marcescit.   The sourest Pear mellows.
Gena pulcherrima senescit.   The hardest disposition relents.
Coma nigerrima canescit.   The tenderest Rose pricks.
Lacertus validissimus rigescit.   The roughest Thorn fences.

Frutices fugiunt vehementissimos ventos.
Specus latent rapidissimas procellas.
Infantes nesciunt mordacissimas curas.
Casæ spernunt minacissimos timores.
Innocentia refellit atrocissima pericula.
Virtus repellit rabiosissimam invidiam.

The winds toss the hugest ships.
Tempests tumble the highest Towers.
Cares vex the loftiest Lords.
Fears disquiet the richest Palaces.
Dangers surround the strongest Forts.
Envy assaults the most illustrious Vertue.

Sunt violæ suaves: Pietas suavissima res est:
    Suavibus est violis suavior alma fides.
Sunt gemmæ pulchræ: Probitas pulcherrima res est,
    Est pulchris gemmis pulchrior alma fides.

Observ. 1. *Adjectives if put alone, understand*

in the	Masculine,	Man.
	Feminine,	Woman.
	Neuter,	Thing.

Sapiens quærit scientiam.   Omnes appetunt bonum.
Justus despicit quæstum.   Plerique quærunt utile.
Fortis adit pericula.   Multi sequuntur jucundum.
Temperatus frænat cupiditates. Pauci colunt honestum.

                                    Lenia

Lenia jejunus poscit. Satur acria quærit.
Æger amara bibit. Dulcia sanus edit.
Lætos læta juvant. Delectant tristia tristes.
Sæva probant sævi. Mitia mitis amat.

Jucundum est sperare. Utile est legere.
Jucundius est potiri. Utilius est scribere.
Jucundissimum est frui. Utilissimum est scire.

Honestum est flectere equum. Æquum est monere pravos.
Decorum est tendere arcum. Justum est coercere superbos.

Turpe est ignorare litteras. Humanum est efferre funus.
Belluinum est damnare Artes. Pium est nudos vestire.

Observ. 2. *Adjectives in the Genitive understand,* Officium.

Sapientis est quærere scientiam.
Fortis est adire pericula.
Justi est despicere avaritiam.
Temperati est frænare cupiditates.

Observ. 3. *The Superlative puts the general Noun in the Genitive.*

Sol   Fulgidissimus syderum.
Aurum   est Pretiosissimum metallorum.
Leo   Generosissimus ferarum.
Adamas   Firmissimus gemmarum.

The *Rose*   *sweetest*   *Flowers.*
     Oak   is the *solidest* of *Trees.*
     whale   *hugest*   *Fishes.*
     Eagle   *swiftest*   *Birds.*

Praxis.

Praxis I. NOminative and Verb agree in Number.
II. The Substantive Verbs Sum, Fio, and Passives Dicor, Appellor, draw a Nominative after them.

III. Of after a Noun is a token of the Genitive Case.

IV. A Noun following a Verb, is of the Accusative Case.

V. To and For (the use of another) are tokens of the Dative Case.

VI. With or By an Instrument, is token of the Ablative Case.

VII. The latter of two Verbs, is of the Infinitive Mood.

VIII. The Preposition requires a Noun in the due Case.

IX. Substantive and Adjective agree in Gender, Case and Number.

X. Then after a Comparative, is a token of the Ablative Case.

The Recapitulatory Exercise.

I. LAbors end, Money abides.
II. Money is a safeguard, Money is called a Queen.

III. Money is a help of Vertue.

IV. Money gains Friends.

V. Liberality scatters Money to the poor, Providence gathers Money for Children.

VI. Money is purchased by Labor.

VII.

VII. *Money is wont to overcome strength.*

VIII. *Contentedness* { *seeks* } *Money* { *greediness.* }
{ *keeps* } *without* { *carefulness.* }

X. *Money is a strong safeguard.*

X. *A penny in the Purse is surer then a Friend in the Court.*

I, **M**Oneys run, *Art sticks.*

II. *Art is an estate.*

III. *Poverty is the Nurse of Arts.*

IV. *Art finishes Nature.*

V. *Fathers provide Arts for Children.*

VI. *Art is finished by Practice.*

VII. *A Theif can rob Moneys.*

VIII. *Art abides among Theeves, in banishment, after losses.*

IX. *Art is a safe estate.*

X. *Art is an estate, safer then Moneys.*

ADverbs *of quantity and quality have the same degrees of comparison as their Adjectives.*

Puer bonis moribus {
Studet diligenter.
Ludit moderatè.
Legit clarè, distinctè, promptè.
Loquitur opportunè, modestè, appositè.
Juvat condiscipulum libenter.
Salutat hospitem humaniter.
}

The { *Comparative* } *is formed by* { *turning* er, è } *into* { ius. }
{ *Superlative* } { } { issimè. }
rè *from the Adjective in* er errimè.

Benè,

Benè, meliùs, optimè.   Valdè, magis, maximè.
Malè, pejus, peſſimè.   Parum, minùs, minimè.
  Multum, plus, plurimum.

Ceſſator ⎰ Valdè ⎱cupit⎰ luctari.
         ⎪ Magis ⎰   ⎱ ſaltare.
         ⎪ Maximè ⎰   ⎰ jactare pilam.
         ⎪ Benè luctatur.
         ⎪ Melius ſaltat.
         ⎨ Optimè jactat pilam.
         ⎪ Parum ⎰   ⎰ legere.
         ⎪ Minùs ⎰curat⎱ ſcribere.
         ⎪ Minimè ⎰   ⎰ componere dictamen.
         ⎪ Malè legit.
         ⎪ Pejùs ſcribit.
         ⎩ Peſſimè componit dictamen.

There are other Adverbs which are not compared.

Non ver perpetuum eſt : Non eſt ſyncera voluptas.
  Nulli non inter gaudia cura venit.
Haud ſine ſente roſa eſt. Nux haud ſine cortice creſcit,
  Æſtivi ſoles haud ſine nube micant.
Non eſt ſemper hyems : Non vexant uſque procellæ
  Nautas, æternâ non nive canet humus.
Haud benè mortales inflantur tempore læto,
  Rebus in adverſis haud malè ſperat homo.

Undique circumſtant humanam incommoda vitam.
  Sæpe fames cruciat : Copia ſæpe necat.
Immodicos ſequitur plerumque ſuperbia cenſus,
  Parvula vix recipit grandia vela ratis.
Pœne per æratas turres excurrit egeſtas,
  Rarò timet leges imperioſa fames.

Frangit membra labor.   Corrumpunt otia mentem.
  Fallax inſidias hoſtis utrinque locat,
Vir vigil in ſortem clypeum prætentat utramque
  Prudenter, Dextrè vir vigil arma movet.

        The Formation of the Pretertenſe.
        Theſe double the head repeating a by e.

                                        Do,

Do, Sto, Mordeo, Spondeo, Pendeo, Tondeo, Pango.
Tango, Cædo, Cado, Parco, Pario, Cano, Fallo,
Cello, Pello, Tendo, Pendo, Pedo, Pepedi,
Disco, Posco, Tundo, Pungo, Curro cucurri.

are avi,   Lavo }   Seno, Tono, Domo, Mico, Plico, Frico }
but   Juvo } vi.   Seco, Neco, Veto, Crepo, Nexo, Cubo } ui.

êre ui,   Neo, Fleo, Vieo, - pleo, - leo, evi - veo, vi.
but   Maneo mansi, Jubeo jussi,
       L and r before - ceo - geo make it si.
       Ardeo, Rideo, Suadeo, Hæreo, Torqueo si.
       Augeo, Frigeo, Luceo, Lugeo xi.
       Sedeo, Prandeo, Strideo, Video di.

ire ivi,   Venio veni, Sancio, Vincio xi.
but   Haurio, Sentio, Sarcio, Parcio, Fulcio, Sepio si.
       Amicio-cui—xi. Salio --ui---ii.

ere, thus   Vinco, Linquo, Scindo, Findo, Fundo, Rumpo loose m,n.
         Ago, Facio, Jacio, Capio make e, Frango, Tango loose n too.
         Lego, Edo, Emo, Fodio, Fugio, lengthen their Vowel.
         c q g h & make xi. rg si. sc vi. Vivo, Struo, Fluo xi.
         mn p b make psi, Lambo, Bibo, Scabo bi. Strepo pui.
         Cedo, Premo, Uro, Gero, Quatio ssi.
         d { Claudo, Plaudo, Rado, --vado, Lædo, Ludo, Rodo,
            { Trudo, Divido si.
            { Cudo, Rudo, Sido, Strido, & nd, di.
         L m n r s t x, in these insert u, Colo, Molo, Volo, Alo.
         Consule, Occulo, Fremo, Gemo, Tremo, Vomo, Gigne
           genui.
         Pono posui. Sero, Pinso, Sterto, Meto messui, Texo texui,
         else Sallo, Psallo li. Vello, velli, & vulsi.
         Como, Promo, Sumo, Demo psi.
         Sino sivi, Lino levi, Cerno crevi, Sperno sprevi, Sterno
           stravi.
         Sero sevi, Quæro quæsivi, Tero trivi, Verro verri.
         Arcesso, Lacesso, ivi. Facesso, Capesso ivi & i. Incesso,
           Viso i.
         Verto i, Peto ivi, Mitto misi, Sisto stiti.

—vo vi, Lacio lexi, Specio xi, Rapio ui, Sapio ui & ivi,
Cupio ivi.
—uo ui. Pluo pluvi.

The *Compound Preters do not double the head except* Diſco,
Poſco, Do. *Theſe put in* u. Antecello, Præcello, Excello,
Compeſco, Diſpeſco, Occino, Succino, Elicio : *But* Incumbo,
&c. omit in alſo Intelligo, Aperio, Operio, Diligo,
Negligo, exi.

—*does not double the head nor change* a *into* e.

The Preter Participle	does loſe n further from	Strinxi Pinxi Finxi Minxi Pinſui Rinxi	ui vi	from	uo vo	make utus.

d — *four,* fidi, fodi, ſcidi, ſedi ſſus, *but* dedi datus. Pandi
    panſus & ſſus.
l — *but* tuli latus.
r — *make* ſus. *But* Peperi partus.
s — *but* torſi, hauſi, fulſi, farſi, ſarſi, indulſi, uſſi, geſſi tus,
    miſi ſſus.   (pſi *makes* ptus.
t — *but* ſteti ſtatus.
   Nexi, Pexi, Flexi, Plexi, Fixi, Fluxi xus.

The Preter Participle compound.

Jactus, factus, captus, raptus, fartus, partus, ſparſus, cantus,
carptus, *turn* a *into* e. Status, ſatus *into* i. *So* cognitus,
agnitus.

The Preter-tenſe of Deponents.

Adipiſcor adeptus.
Amplector amplexus.
Comminiſcor commentus.
Complector complexus.
Expergiſcor experrectus.
Fruor fruitus.
Fungor functus ſum.
Gradior greſſus,

Iraſcor iratus.
Labor lapſus.
Loquor loquutus.
Morior mortuus.
Nanciſcor nactus.
Naſcor natus.
Nitor niſus & xus.
Obliviſcor oblitus.

               Orior

Orior ortus.	Queror queſtus.
Paciſcor paďus.	Sequor ſequutus.
Patior paſſus.	Ulciſcor ultus.
Proficiſcor profeďus.	Utor uſus.

Divertor, Prævertor, Revertor, borrow the Preter tenſe Aďive.

In the ſecond long, Fateor faſſus, Confiteor confeſſus, Miſereor miſertus, Reor ratus, Tueor tuitus.

In the third long, Aſſentior aſſenſus, Metior menſus, Experior, Opperior, Comperior --pertus. Ordior *to weave* orditus, *to begin* orſus *with the Compounds.*

The Preter-tenſe of Neuter-Paſſives.

Audeo auſus, Gaudeo gaviſus, Fido fiſus, Fio faďus, Mœreo mœſtus, Soleo ſolitus.

Theſe want the firſt theam; Cœpi, Odi, Memini.

Theſe want the ſecond theam; Polleo, Renideo, Gliſco, Fatiſco, Vergo, Ambigo, *and Denominative Inceptives, as* Pueraſco.

Theſe want the Preter-Participle, Lambo, Scabo, Mico, Parco, Diſpeſco, Compeſco, Poſco, Diſco, Strido, Rudo, Aveo, Paveo, Flaveo, Liveo, Conniveo, Ferveo, Satago, Dego, Ango, Lingo, Ningo, Sugo, Pſallo, Volo, Nolo, Malo, Tremo. *Compounds of* Nuo, *and Compounds of* Cado, *beſides* Occido *and* Recido, Timeo, Metuo, Reſpuo, Linquo, Luo, Cluo, Sterto. Ingruo, Congruo, *and Neuters in* eo, ui, *except* Oleo, Doleo, Placeo, Taceo, Jacceo, Noceo, Pareo, Careo, Pateo, Lateo, Valeo, Caleo.

There are accounted eighteen Pronouns.

> Ego, Tu, Sui,
> Meus, Tuus,
> Noſter, Veſter,
>   Suus,
> Quis? Qui,
> Is, Iſte, Ille.
> Hic, Ipſe,
> Cujas? Noſtras, Veſtras,

Singulariter·

Singulariter
- N. Ego.
- G. Mei.
- Acc. Me.
- D. Mihi.
- Abl. Me.

Pluraliter
- N. Nos.
- G. Noſtrum î.
- Acc. Nos.
- D. } Nobis.
- Abl. }

Singulariter
- N. Tu.
- G. Tui.
- Acc. Te.
- D. Tibi.
- Abl. Te.

Pluraliter
- N. Vos.
- G. Veſtrum î.
- Acc. Vos.
- D. } Vobis.
- Abl. }

Singulariter & Pluraliter
- N.
- G. Sui.
- Acc. Se.
- D. Sibi.
- Abl. Se.

Sui & Suus *are interpreted by the forenamed ſubject.*

Pater }
Mater } ſolatur } ſe ſuis liberis.
Parentes ſolantur }
Urbs ſolatur ſe ſuis civibus.

Theſe ſix make their Neuter in d, Quis, Quæ, Quid, (*but* Qui, Quæ, Quod) Is, Ea, Id, Iſte, Iſta, Iſtud, Ille, Illa, Illud. *And* Alius, a, ud.

Singulariter
- N. Quis, quæ, quid.
- G. Cujus.
- Acc. Quem, quam.
- D. Cui.
- Abl. Quo î, quâ.

Pluraliter
- N. Qui, quæ, quæ.
- G. Quorum, quarum.
- Acc. Quos, quas.
- D. } Quibus *or* queis.
- Abl. }

Singulariter
- N. Hic, hæc, hoc.
- G. Hujus.
- Acc. Hunc, hanc.
- D. Huic.
- Abl. Hoc, hâc.

Pluraliter
- N. Hi, hæ, hæc.
- G. Horum, harum.
- Acc. Hos, has.
- D. } His.
- Abl. }

Singulariter
- N. Is, ea, id.
- G. Ejus.
- Acc. Eum, eam.
- D. Ei.
- Abl. Eo, eâ.

Pluraliter
- N. Ii, eæ, ea.
- G. Eorum, earum.
- Acc. Eos, eas.
- D. } Iis.
- Abl. }

E   Singulariter

Singulariter
{
N. Ifte, ifta, iftud.
G. Iftius.
Acc. Iftum, iftam.
D. Ifti.
Abl. Ifto â.
}

Pluraliter
{
N. Ifti, iftæ, ifta.
G. Iftorum, iftarum.
Acc. Iftos, iftas.
D.
Abl. } Iftis.
}

So Ille. Alius *makes in the* G. Sing. Alîus, D. Alii. *But* Ipfe, a, um,

& {
Unus, ullus, nullus, folus, totus, } *make the* G. Sing.
Uter ? uterque, neuter, alteruter, } ius, D. i.
}

Alter *makes the* Gen. Sing. Alterîus.

The perfons fpeaking and fpoken to, have their form.

Obfervo, Innuo, Irafcor, Vociferor.
Cur ludis ? cur ceffas ? cur torpes ?
Cur nugaris ?

The Pronoun *is added for diftinction, or eminence, and fin-gularity.*

Ego {
Lego.
Rogo.
Meditor.
Studeo.
Laudor.
Promoveor.
Donor.
}

Tu {
Ludis.
Ceffas.
Nugaris.
Rides.
Objurgaris.
Teneris.
Caftigaris.
}

Nouns in us *have a* Vocative *termination in* e, *except* Deus. Meus *makes* mi, Filius fili. *And all proper names in* ius *make* i. Georgius Georgi.

Of what Number the Vocative *is, the* Imperative *is of the fame.*

Puer {
Sede in loco tuo.
Lege librum tuum.
Examina lectionem tuam.
Audi condifcipulum tuum.
}

Pueri

Pueri ⎧ Parate chartam veſtram.
⎨ Adhibete elementa veſtra.
⎨ Expedite dictionarium veſtrum.
⎩ Conjungite voces ſingulas.

The Vocative is ſet diſtinct in the ſentence.

A. Quem librum legis, mi puer ? B. Sententias Pueriles, domine. A. Quotâ in claſſe ſedes ? B. In ſecundâ. A. Nihilne Colloquiorum ſuaviſſime, didicit claſſis veſtra ? B. Jam nunc, domine, tendimus ad Confabulatiunculas, & Corderii Colloquia. Hactenus hæremus in Rudimentis. A. Feliciter ; vale, blandum caput. B. Valebis tu quoque vir ſumme.

The Interrogative and Reſponſive are made by the ſame Caſe.

A. Quid eſt illud in ſinu tuo, mi puer ? B. Liber, Domine. A. Cujus eſt iſte liber ? B. Condiſcipuli mei. A. Quem condiſcipulum vis ? B. Ducem Scholæ noſtræ. A. Cui ſtudio te addicis ? B. Grammaticæ. A. Quotâ in claſſe ſedes ? B. Secundâ. A. Libet ulterius percontari. Quarum rerum omnes mortales meminiſſe oportet ? B. Mortis, judicii, cœli, inferni. A. Quarum rerum eoſdem obliviſci decet ? B. Injuriarum, convitiorum, offenſarum. A. Quas opes maximas opinari poſſumus ? B. Contentum ſuis rebus animum. A. Quem theſaurum pauperes ſortiuntur ? B. Laborem. A. Cui rei debemus imprimis parcere ? B. Tempori. A. Quibus cum hominibus verſari licet ? B. Cum omnibus. A. Qualibus amicis uti convenit ? B. Probis. A. Quanti fas eſt exiſtimationem hominum de nobis bonam facere ? B. Permagni. A. Quanti pecuniam æſtimare nefas eſt ? B. Pluris. A. Quotus quiſque ſic animatus eſt ? B. Vix decimus quiſque. A. Quænam eſt radix malorum omnium ? B. Avaritia. A. Cui ætati vitium hoc potiſſimùm inſidiari jamdiu obſervatum eſt ? B. Senectuti. A. Quâ labe maculatur adoleſcentia ? B. Amore voluptatum. A. Ecquod veneum eſt pueritiæ dulce ? B. Otium. A. Quot annos natus es ? B. Octo. A. Quotum ætatis annum agis ? B. Nonum. A. Aptè reſpondiſti, puer ingenue, abi, vir es.

E 2

I. *Pronouns are signs for things otherwise named.*
I I. *The person speaking and spoken to have their form.*
I I I. *Of what number the Vocative is, the Imperative is of the same.*
I V. *The Vocative is set distinct in the sentence.*
V. *The Interrogative and Responsive are made by the same Case.*

I. Mors conjungitur cum ipsâ vitâ. Hæc præcedit illam, I'la sequitur hanc.
I I. Novi natalem. Nescio diem mortis.
I I I. Suspicite mortem, juvenes. Aspicite eandem, senes.
I V. Mors vos, juvenes, rapit : Eadem vos, Senes, colligit.
V. A. Quorum mors est acerba ? B. Juvenum. A. Quorum mors est matura ? B. Senum.

Nænia. I. Opus est faciendum, quis faciet ? I I. Que faciet ? I I I. Opus est factum, quis fecit ? Lapis, jactus, jecit ? Vitrum, fractum, fregit ? Opus, actum, egit ? I V. A. Quota est hora ? B. Instat, prima, secunda. C. Sonat, tertia, quarta. D. Audita est, quinta, sexta. E. Præteriit cum quadrante, septima, octava. F. Est sesqui, nona, decima. G. Præteriit cum dodrante, undecima, duodecima. V. Quid ubi fit ? VI. Quando ? VII. Quamdiu ?

PRAXIS. I.

Subſtantives are joyned in the ſame caſe, as, Sirnames, names of dignity, age, trade, relation, diſcriptions plain, or in likeneſs onely and definitions.

Marcus, Tullius, Cicero, } eſt autor { de Officiis.
Publius, Ovidius, Naſo, } libri { Triſtium.

Cicero { Conſul Romanus / Vir egregius / Orator diſertiſſimus / Oratorum facilè princeps / Flumen eloquentiæ } appellatur filius fullonis.

Ro ſa

Rosa, laus florum citè arescit.
Leo, terror nemorum tandem moritur.
Boletus, deliciæ mensarum crescunt in campis.
Urticæ, labes hortorum diligenter evellitur.

PRAXIS II.

THe Relative receives { Gender and Number { Case } from (2)

(2) the { Noun foregoing } immediately the Nominative { Verb following } with a Nom. the after Verb.

Monetarius cudit pecuniam { quæ pascit avaritiam. { quam avaritia devorat.

Fusor fundit typos { qui instruunt typographum. { duos typographus emit.

Muri cingunt urbem { quæ continet opifices. { quam opifices incolunt.

Sepes tuetur agrum { qui fert fruges. { quem fruges operiunt.

Onus gravat humeros { qui subeunt sarcinam. { quos sarcina premit.

Doctrina levat animum { quem præcepta imbuunt. { qui recipit præcepta.

The Dyer dies the Purple which { adorns the Magistrate. { the Magistrate wears.

The Printer Prints the Books which { delight the Scholar. { the Scholar reads.

E 3   Rivers

Rivers water the Ground which {
enſnares heats.
the heats chap.

Props ſuſtain the Vine which {
produces Cluſters.
the Cluſters load.

Comfort raiſes the Minde which {
diſcovers cares.
cares diſquiet.

Honor cloaths the Breſt which {
deſires Learning.
Learning poſſeſſes.

A Dyer buys a Copper, which the Brazier ſells.
The Clothier buys the Wooll, which the Shepherd ſells.
The Merchant buys the Cloaths, which the Cloathier ſells.
A Scholar buys the Books, which the Bookſeller ſells.

A Barber buys a Raſor, which ſhaves a Beard.
A Mower buys a Sythe, which cuts the Meadows.
The Carpenter buys a Hatchet, which hews Timber.
The Traveller buys a Sword, which defends life.

Avari defodiunt aurum, quod foſſor effodit.
Sartor diſcindit pannum, quem textor contexit.
Tinctor inſicit veſtem, quam fullo lavat.
Molitor comminuit triticum, quod tritor excutit.

Scintilla creat flammam, quæ incendit urbem.
Rima admittit aquam, quæ mergit navem.
Rima emittit potum, qui lavat pavimentum.
Porrigo diffundit venenum, quod pervadit gregem.

Hunger cureth the niceneſs, which fulneſs breeds.
Diſcipline removes the contempt, which familiarity draws.
Diſuſe looſeth the art, which uſe gains.
Idleneſs conſumeth the wealth, which labor gets.
The File poliſheth the Iron, which the Ruſt frets.

Clementia frangit animos, quos aſperitas irritat.
Submiſſio pacat iram, quam contumacia provocat.
Verecundia ornat puerum, quem improbitas dehoneſtat.
Somnus reparat vires, quas labor exhauſit.
Pax recludit portas, quas bellum claudit.

The

The *Farmer Tills* the *Field*, *which feeds the Farmer.*
The *Shepherd feeds the Flock*, *which feeds the Shepherd.*
A Man keeps a Horse, which carries a man.
The *old Man bears up the staff*, *which bears up the old Man.*
The *Thief robs the Judge*, *which condemns the Thief.*

Glacies parit aquam, quæ parit glaciem.
Semen emittit arborem, quæ emittit semen.
Nox præcedit lucem, quæ præcedit noctem.
Sitis intendit hydropem, qui intendit sitim.
Mæror inducit solitudinem, quæ inducit mœrorem.

Observe, *For the Latine Composition oftentimes the Ante-*
cedent being pitched down, the rest of the principal sentence
is thrown behinde the Relative Sentence, as

Pecuniam $\begin{cases} \text{quæ pascit avaritiam,} \\ \text{quam avaritia devorat,} \end{cases}$ monetarius cudit.

Zibethum, quod $\begin{cases} \text{aspergit aulicos ,} \\ \text{aulici olent,} \end{cases}$ felis excernit.

Succinum, quod $\begin{cases} \text{delectat sumptuosos,} \\ \text{sumptuosi hauriunt,} \end{cases}$ mare evomit.

Or the Antecedent is blended with the Relative sentence, as

Quas eques induit ocreas, sutor ungit.
Quos Rex gestat calceos, sutor conficit.
Quibus scholaris utitur libris, Bibliopola vendit.

The Relative sentence is alike depending on the Nominative
of the Principal.

Somnus, quem divites ambiunt, ambit pauperes.
Laus, quam gloriosi affectant, affectat modestos.
Præmium, quod pigri petunt, petit impigros.
Dignitas, quam ambitiosi sequuntur, sequitur probos.

Observ. *whose, whereof, whereto, wherewith. whereby,*
wherein are Relative Obliques of both Numbers.

E 4   PRAXIS

PRAXIS III.

P *Articiples govern the Case of their Verb.*

Arator premens stivam
Nauta gubernans clavum
Pileo cogens lanas
Sutor suens calceos } quæritat victum.
Faber dolans trabem
Sector secans tabulas

A {
Soldier managing a Sword
Clark handling a Pen
Printer Printing Books
Gardiner Planting Trees } *obtaineth praise.*
Lawyer pleading Causes
Physician prescribing Medicines
}

Puer {
Verberans turbinem flagello
Percutiens pilam reticulo
Projiciens lapidem fundâ } ludit.
Contorquens glandem ballistâ
}

A Clark {
Cutting a Pen with a Pen-Knife
Ruling Paper with a Ruler
Writing Letters with Ink } *sits.*
Drying the Copy with Sand
}

Light discovering the World, covers the Sun.
The Sun softning Wax, hardens Clay.

Nox arcens homines evocat feras.
Dies evocans homines arcet feras.

Miles aditurus aciem
Messor resecturus segetem
Fossor ducturus fossam } emit {
Sartor sarturus vestes
Sutor suturus calceos

{ gladium.
talcem.
ligonem.
acum.
subulam.

A {
Barber about to shave Beards
Carpenter about to square Timber
Sawyer about to saw Boards } buys {
Cloathier about to make Cloaths
Scholar about to get Wisdom

{ *a Rasor.*
an Ax.
a Saw.
Wooll.
Books.

Turbo

Turbo verberandus flagello
Pila percutienda reticulo
Lapis projiciendus fundâ
Glans contorquenda ballistâ } sumitur à puero.

A Pen-Knife
A Pen
Paper
A Copy } to be { nhetted with a Horn,
ut with a Pen-Knife,
ruled with a Ruler,
dryed with Sand, } is taken by a Clark.

Pratum flumine rigandum. in valle subsidit.
Vinea sole fovenda in collibus hæret.

Corpús fractum diurnis laboribus reficitur nocturnâ quiete.
Pectus hebetatum immodicis studiis recreatur tempestivo otio.
Appetitus dejectus suavibus cibis renovatur acri aceto.
Animus inflatus perpetuis successibus reprimitur diversâ forte.

The Earth chap'd with Summer-heat, is moyslened with Autumnal showres.
The Rivers bound with Winter frosts, are thawed with Spring gales.
A Ship tost with vehement storms, is recovered with a gentle wind.
A Country afflicted with long War, is restored with sweet Peace.

——*ing with the mark of a Case is a Gerund from* ——*dus.*

Cupiditas { edendi
bibendi
dormiendi
indendi } augetur { edendo.
bibendo.
dormiendo.
ludendo.

The skill of { *Swimming*
Riding
Running
Leaping } *is got by* { *Swimming.*
Riding.
Running.
Leaping.

Usus { Legendi
Scribendi
Canendi
Numerandi } reddit promptos ad { Legendum.
Scribendum.
Canendum.
Numerandum.

The

The practice of { Spinning / Weaving / Burling / Shearing } makes active at { Spinning. / Weaving. / Burling. / Shearing. }

The Noun put after the Gerund, may also, and is more usually joyned in Concord with it; and it is then called a Gerundive Adjective.

Magister { hortatur puerum ad { Legendam lectionem. / Scribendum dictamen. } / prohibet à { Lacerando libro. / Scindendis vestibus. } }

Scientia gubernandi populi continetur { Moderandis perturbationibus. / Vincendis cupiditatibus. }

The skill of exercising valor is tryed by { bearing afflictions. / despising pleasures. }

Wisdom { exhorts men to { flee Vice. / desire Vertue. } / dehorts from { deserting Justice. / committing Injury. } }

Serta relaturus certamina dura lacessit,
Displicet è facili palma petita jugo.

Dulcia privatæ fugiens solatia vitæ,
Arctius acclivi tramite scandit iter.

Arte levi navem tranquilla per æquora vectam,
Dirigit in tumidis nauta peritus aquis.

Pellentem morbos, non mollis vestis, & aurum
Arguit, at medicum pestis & aura gravis.

A Verbal of the Participle of the Preter tense is used in the Accusative and Ablative; called the former and latter Supine.

The

The latter of two Verbs, if the former be a Verb of Moti-
on, is put into the first Supine.

Puer it
$\begin{cases}\text{oratum, lotum manus \& os.}\\\text{jentatum, petitum aliquid.}\\\text{repetitum lectionem, pranfum.}\\\text{fcriptum, lufum, cænatum.}\\\text{mictum, feceffum, cubitum, dormitum.}\end{cases}$

The Infinitive Paffive, after Adjectives may be exprefl by
the latter Supine.

Hoc eft
$\begin{cases}\text{Honeftum}\\\text{Turpe}\end{cases}$
$\begin{cases}\text{Vifu.}\\\text{Auditu.}\\\text{Dictu.}\\\text{Factu.}\end{cases}$

PRAXIS IV.

ABfolute *Sentences are put in the Ablative Cafe.*

Tinnunculo plangente, fuccumbunt alaudæ,
Catulis latrantibus, cervi fugiunt,
Leone rugiente, feræ expavefcunt.
Gallo canente, diluculum appropinquat.

The Trumpet founding, the Horfe neighs.
The whale fwimming, the Sea boyls.
The Swallows coming, the Summer approaches.
The Flies departing, cold haftens.

Suavè rofæ redolent, Zephyro fpirante per hortum.
Lilia formofùm, fole micante, nitent.
Vere tepente, jacit blandas Philomela querelas.
Concretæ, Boreâ flante, gelantur aquæ.
Singula diverfis tribuuntur tempora formis,
Alternas certâ lege regente vices.

Being *put abfolutely, is of the Preter tenfe Paffive.*

Work being finifhed, reft is welcome :
Cares being fcattered, the minde is quiet.

Having

Having *with a Transitive Verb, puts it into the Participle of the Preter tense Absolute.*

The Husbandman having unyoked the Oxen, returns to the Village.

The School-Master having dismissed the Scholars, walks into the Field.

Aves, relicto nido, quærunt escam.
Mercator, exactâ peregrinatione, reportat opes.

If that Transitive be rendered by a Deponent, it is fashioned by the Rule of Participal dependent Sentences.

Verus amicus opitulatus misero, gratulatur felici.
Amicus infidus adulatus diviti, deserit pauperem.

Discipulus ludit, clausis in scrinia libris,
    Sepositis armis, otia miles agit.

Nautæ, subductis in littora tuta carinis,
    Hiberni vitant murmura rauca freti.

Observ. *Thus also absolute Sentences are pricked into the principal one, as* Pueri, Magistro Scholam ingresso, sedent taciti.

Tenebræ, sole orto, diffugiunt.

PRAXIS V.

Conjunctions *Copulative, joyn like Signs (where different are not expreſt)*

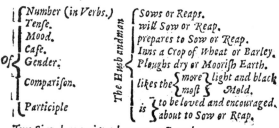

Number (*in Verbs.*)		*Sows or Reaps.*
Tense.		*will Sow or Reap.*
Mood.		*prepares to Sow or Reap.*
Case.		*Inns a Crop of Wheat or Barley.*
Of ⎨ Gender.	*The Husbandman*	*Ploughs dry or Moorish Earth.*
Comparison.		*likes the* ⎨ *more* ⎬ *light and black* ⎨ *most* ⎬ *Mold.*
Participle		*is* ⎨ *to be loved and encouraged.* ⎬ *about to Sow or Reap.*

Two Singulars conjoyned, govern a Plural.
    Dolor & voluptas alternantur.

Observ.

Obſerv. *In more terms than two heaped together, the for-*
mer are put unconjoynedly with a pauſe between, onely the con-
junction is expreſt to the two laſt. Piſtores, Lanii, Cetarii,
& Popinones eſculenta vendunt. Tinctores, Carminatores,
Nctores, Textores, Fullones, Defloccatores, & Panniton-
ſores pannum præparant. *In Rhetorical ſtile of Proſe or Verſe*
ſometimes all are conjoyned to cauſe deliberation, and to
magnifie: Inconſtantes homines & ſperant, & timent; &
optant, & fugiunt *(called* Polyſyndeton.) *Other times all*
are left looſe to ſignifie expedition: Inconſtantes ſperant, timent, optant, fugiunt, *(called* Aſyndeton.)

Note ſecondly, Conjunctions couple like Caſes.

$$
\left.\begin{array}{l} \text{Hora abit} \\ \text{Ætas deſluit} \\ \text{Vita pendet} \end{array}\right\} \text{inter} \left\{\begin{array}{l} \text{Speculum} \\ \text{Ludum} \\ \text{Spem} \end{array}\right\} \& \left\{\begin{array}{l} \text{Pectinem.} \\ \text{Somnum.} \\ \text{Metum.} \end{array}\right.
$$

Præpone animam ſcilicet gemmam.
Poſtpone corpus videlicet ciſtam.
Excole meliorem partem, h. e. mentem.

$$
\left.\begin{array}{l} \text{Gemma} \\ \text{Bellum} \\ \text{Nemo} \end{array}\right\} \text{eſt} \left\{\begin{array}{l} \text{Vilior quàm ſapientia.} \\ \text{Mitius quàm luxuria.} \\ \text{Beatus niſi ſapiens.} \end{array}\right.
$$

Parce tempori perinde ac theſauro.
Excute mærorem tanquam tineam animi.
Fuge deſidiam velut lupum.

Omnia poſſunt eripi præcerquam dotes animi.
Homo pro factis reportat lætitiam vel mœrorem.
Geſſator conſequitur nec honorem nec opes.
Pauper conſultat malitne laborem an egeſtatem.

Some Conjunctions require a Subjunctive Mood, as Ut, uti,
(that) Utinam, ne, quin; *others ordinarily admit a Sub-*
junctive, ni, ſi, niſi, quòd, cùm.
Jubeo ut, uti facias officium.

Utinam

Utinam {
legas ! perlegas ! difcas ! edifcas !
fedeas in loco tuo ! loquaris ! eloquaris !
exponas, examines, repetas lectionem tuam !
juves condifcipulos tuos !
facias officium, puer !
}

Si facias hæc omnia benè eft : Sin ludas, ceffes, rideas, garrias ; grave imminet periculum.

Moneo ne ludas, ceffes, exclames, lucteris, nugèris.

Non potes quin aliud agas.

Nifi facias officium vapulabis.

Quòd, *Becaufe*

Tht {
Father rejoyces
Mafter grieves
Phyfician mourns
} because the {
Son loves Vertue.
Scholar affects idlenefs.
Patient defpifes directions
}

Cum {
tinnunculus plangat, alaudæ fuccumbunt.
catuli latrent, cervi fugiunt.
leo rugiat, feræ ex pavefcunt.
gallus canat, diluculum appropinquat.
}

When the {
Trumpet founds, the Horfe neighs.
Whale fwims, the Sea boyls.
Swallows come, Summer approaches.
Flies depart, cold haftens.
}

Obferv. *Conjunctive Sentences are alfo pricked in between the parts of the principal fentence.*

Celligere folet medicus, dum ver præbet, rofas: Quas, ubi Sol torruerit agros, fruftra requirit æger.

Quærere debet puer, dum anni finunt, literas: quas, ubi curæ domefticæ circumfteterint, vir incaffum defiderabit.

Omnia lege rotant, fi cœli fydera fpectes :
Seu terram fpectes, omnia lege vigent :
Sive maris liquidos pinnato cum grege campos
Perfpicias, certâ nil nifi lege fluit.

Cum Sol abfcedat, nudatur frondibus arbor
Cum Sol accedat, gramine terra viret.

Lux

Lux parit alma diem, ne tempora pigra quiescant :
Neve cadant vires, nox tegit atra polum.

Ordine cuncta geruntur, & ordine cuncta reguntur,
Omnia lege fluunt : Nil sine lege ruit.

PRAXIS VI.

THe Present and Preter of the Subjunctive without a Conjunction is to be rendred Imperatively for the most part, the other Tenses potentially.

Qui cupit laudem, studeat, discat, legat, scribat.

Let
{
the Grashoppers sing, the Ant will labor.
Drones loyter, Bees will work.
Worms crawl, Eagles will flie.
Hares fear, Lyons will fight.
}

Cessator studeret, si posset facere citra laborem.
Studuerit, didicerit, legerit cessator, doctrina sequetur.
Occasio adfuisset nisi mens defuisset.

A Boy
{
would play, if he durst.
would write, if he could.
should repeat, if the form stood out.
could answer, if he were asked.
}

Contexture of Sentences.

1. Several Sentences on the same subject, take it common.

Before the Verb.

Rosa jam rubet, mox marcescit.
Vitrum, dum splendet, frangitur.
Bulla nunc lucet, nunc disparet.
Scintilla modò micat, modò perit.

Amnis mane fluit, vespere refluit.
Ventus hodie flat, cras reflat.
Luna 14 diebus crescit, totidem diebus decrescit.
Frondes vere germinant, autumno decidunt.

which common subject may be added to the last sentence.

Præcipitat linguam : Pugnas committit : Amicos
   Diſſolvit : Mentes obruit ebrietas.

The after Verb.

Segetem terra parit, imber auget.
Triticum tritor excutit, molitor comminuit.
Lanam tondet paſtor, emit pannifex.
Pannos texit textor, tingit tinctor.

Libros imprimit typographus, vendit bibliopola.
Pharmaca præſcribit medicus, miſcet pharmacopola.
Navem texit naupegus, agit nauclerus.
Currum pangit carpentarius, agit auriga.

Ingenium natura facit : Corroborat uſus.
   Excolit ars : Nutrit gloria : Cura polit.

2. Several ſentences on the ſame Verb, take it common.

Solvit ſalem aqua, ceram ignis.
Jungit tabulas gluten, lateres cœmentum.
Conſolidat metalla ferrumen, vulnera unguentum.
Secat vitrum ſmiris, lignum ſecuris.

Tegunt pedes calcei, manus chirothecæ.
Ornat collum torquis, brachium armilla.
Paſcit bovem fœnum, ſuem colluvies.
Sanat hominem medicus, equum veterinarius.

Which Common Verb may be added to the laſt ſentence.

Squammas, piſcis : avis, plumas ; barbam atque capillos,
   Hœdus ; aper, ſetas ; vellera geſtat ovis.

Ver tepidum, ſertis : Maturis frugibus, æſtas :
   Autumnus, pomis : Igne juvatur hyems.

3. Several Adjectives on the ſame Subſtantive take it common ; before or after the Verb.

Puer ignavus ceſſat, ſtudioſus elaborat.
Miles fortis pugnat, piger fugit.
Nauta veteranus audet, novitius pallet.
Equus generoſus currit, degener deficit.

O do

Odor teter offendit, suavis delectat.
Vinum modicum levat, nimium obruit.
Lignum aridum flagrat, viride fumat.
Vestis munda decet, immunda dedecet.

which Common Substantive, may be added to the last sentence.

Tabescit vitiis suprema, laboribus ima ;
  Quae vitae ratio est inter utrumque placet.

Vasa aurea fundit aurifaber ; fictilia fingit figulus.
Vestem laneam vendit pannifex, lineam texit linteo.
Calceos veteres resarcit cerdo ; novos conficit sutor.
Pensum breve discipulus flagitat ; justum praeceptor exigit.

Ætatem teneram nugæ abstrahunt ; Maturam curæ impediunt.
Censum exiguum inopia premit ; ingentem pericula circumstant.
Conditionem humilem obscuritas sepelit, excelsam invidia petit.
Vitam rusticam labores frangunt, urbanam vitia corrumpunt.

Cur, cùm longa dies urbes, cùm marmora salvat,
  Incautos homines tarda senecta premat ?

Tempore quod segetes, quod poma, quod excoquit uvas,
  Cura suas vires ponit, & ira suas.

The Interjections are Notes of Passion.

O *calling,* Heus & O-he, *with a Vocative.*
O *exclaiming, with Nominative, Accusative, and Vocative.*
Proh, Ah, *and* Vah, *with Accusative and Vocative.*
Heu *with an Accusative.*
Hei, mihi. Væ tibi.
Hem manum.
Apage pigritiam.

The Doctrine of Prosodia may be well refer'd to ars Poetica, which with the Substance of Smetius, is briefly and judiciously couched in order by Mr. Adam Littleton.

E

Thus far I have undertaken, either to digest or illustrate the first Rudiments of the Latine Tongue, which may in a short time be comprehended by one of an ordinary capacity and industry. Which Observations I adventure to publick view for my own use, and the ease of those, who shall approve to instruct their yong Scholars to the practise of Latine.

FINIS.

A.

To abide, *Maneo* ere.
   To abound, *Abundo* are.
   Accurate, *Accuratus* i.
An Acorn, *Glans* des.
Active, *Promptus* i.
To adorn, *Orno* are.
To affect. *Afficio* are.
To afflict, *Affligo* ere.
An affliction, *Ærumna* æ.
Ale, *Cervisia* æ.
An Ant, *Formica* æ.
An Apothecary, *Pharmacopola* æ.
To approach, *Appropinquo* are.
An Arch, *Fornix* ices.
An Army, *Exercitus* ûs.
An Arrow, *Sagitta* æ.
Art, *Ars* tes.
An Artist, *Artifex* ices.
To assault, *Impugno* are.
An Ass, *Asinus* i.
To assemble, *Convenio* ire.
An Assembly, *Concio* nes.
Autumnal, *Autumnalis* es.
An Awl, *Subula* æ.
An Ax, *Ascia* æ.

B.

A Ballance, *Libramen* ina.
A Band, *Vinculum* a.
Banishment, *Exilium* a.
A Bank, *Ripa* æ.
A Barb, *Spica* æ.
A Barber, *Tonsor* es.
Barley, *Hordeum* a.

A Battle, *Prælium* a.
A Beam, *Trabs* es.
A Bean, *Faba* æ.
To bear, *Fero* re.
To bear up, *Sustineo* ere.
A Beard, *Barba* æ.
A Beast, *Fera* æ.
A Bee, *Apis* es.
Beer, *Potus* ûs.
A Begger, *Mendicus* i.
A Bell, *Campana* æ.
A Bench, *Subsellium* æ.
To bend, *Tendo* ere.
To binde, *Ligo* are.
A Bird, *Avis* es.
To bite, *Mordeo* ere.
Biting, *Mordax* ces.
Bitter, *Amarus* i.
Black, *Niger* gri.
To blame, *Culpo* are.
To blast, *Deflorefco* ere.
Blew, *Cæruleus* i.
Blood, *Sanguis* ines.
A Blossom, *Flosculus* i.
To blow, *Flo* are.
A Board, *Tabula* æ.
To boyl (Act.) *Coquo* ere. (Neut.)
   Bullio ire.
A Bone, *Os* sa.
A Book, *Liber* bri.
A Bookseller, *Bibliopola* æ.
To bound, *Coerceo* ere.
A Bow, *Arcus* ûs.
A Bow-case, *Corytus* i.
A Bowl, *Calix* ices.
A Boy, *Puer* i.
The Brain, *Cerebrum* a.
Bran, *Furfur* ures.

A

A Brazier, *Ærarius* i.
To break (Act.) *Frango* ere.
 (Neut.) *Crepo* are.
A Brest, *Pectus* ora.
To Bread, *Pario* ere.
A Bricklayer, *Cæmentarius* i.
A Bridle, *Frænum* (i &) a.
Brigh, *Clarus* i.
To bring, *Affero* re.
A Brink, *Margo* ines.
Broad, *Latus* i.
A Brother, *Frater* tres.
To build, *Ædifico* are.
A Bull, *Taurus* i.
A Bulwark, *Agger* es.
To burl, *Enodo* are.
A Burler, *Enodator* es.
To burn (Act.) *Uro* ere. (Neut.)
 Ardeo ere.
To buy, *Emo* ere.

C.

A Cage, *Cavea* æ.
To call, *Voco* are.
A Candle, *Candela* æ.
A Captain, *Dux* ces.
A care, *Cura* æ.
Carefulness, *Sollicitudo* ines.
A Carpenter, *Faber* bri.
To carry, *Veho* ere.
A Carter, *Bubulcus* i.
A Castle, *Castellum* a.
A Cat, *Felis* es.
A Cause, *Causa* æ.
A Cellar, *Cella* æ.
Chaff, *Palea* æ.
To chap, *Findo* ere.
A Chain, *Catena* æ.
A Chamber, *Cubiculum* a.
To charge, *Grassor* ari.

To chear, *Conforto* are.
A Childe, *Puer* i.
A Chimney, *Focus* i.
A Church, *Templum* a.
A City, *Urbs* es.
Clay, *Lutum* a.
Clear, *Clarus* i.
A Clark, *Scriba* æ.
A Client, *Cliens* tes.
A clime, *Plaga* æ.
Cloth, *Pannus* i.
To cloath, *Vestio* ire.
A Clothier, *Pannificus* i.
A Cloth-worker, *Interpolator* es.
Clotty, *Spissus* i.
A Coud, *Nubes* is.
A Cluster, *Racemus* i.
A Cobler, *Cerdo* nes.
A Cock, *Gallus* i.
Cold (Subst.) *Frigus* ora. (Adj.)
 Frigidus i.
To come, *Venio* ire.
Comfort, *Consolatio* nes.
To commit, *Infero* re.
To condemn, *Condemno* are.
A Conqueror, *Victor* es.
To consume, *Consumo* ere.
To contain, *Contineo* ere.
A contempt, *Contemptus* us.
Contentedness, *Æquanimitas* tes
A Cook, *Popino* nes.
To cool (Act.) *Frigefacio* ere
 (Neut.) *Frigesco* ere.
A Copper, *Ahenum* a.
A Copy, *Exemplum* a.
Corn, *Frumentum* a.
To cover, *Tego* ere.
Covetousness, *Avaritia* æ.
A Countrey, *Regio* nes.
A Court, *Aula* æ.
To craul, *Repto* are.

A crime, *Crimen* ina.
A Crop, *Meßis* es.
To crouch, *Cubo* are.
Cruel, *Crudelis* es.
To curb, *Cohibeo* ere.
To cure, *Sano* are.
A Custom, *Consuetudo* ines.
To cut, *Seco* are.

D.

D Anger, *Periculum* a.
 To dare, *Audeo* ere.
Dark, *Tenebrosus* i.
To darken, *Obscuro* are.
A date, *Dactylus* i.
A day, *Dies* ès.
Death, *Mors* tes.
Deep, *Profundus* i.
To defend, *Tueor* eri.
To dehort, *Dehortor* ari.
Delicate, *Lautus* i.
To delight, *Delecto* are.
To depart, *Discedo* ere.
To desert, *Desero* ere.
To desire, *Cupio* ere.
To despise, *Sperno* ere.
Difficult, *Difficilis* es.
A difficulty, *Difficultas* tes.
To dig, *Fodio* ere.
A direction, *Præscriptum* a.
Discipline, *Disciplina* æ.
Discord, *Discordia* æ.
To discover, *Prodo* ere.
To discourse, *Dissero* ere.
A disease, *Morbus* i.
Disgrace, *Dedecus* ora.
A Dish, *Ferculum* a.
To dismiss, *Dimitte* ere.
A disposition, *Ingenium* a,
To disquiet, *Inquieto* are.

Disuse, *Desuetudo* ines.
A Ditch, *Fossa* æ.
A Ditcher, *Fossor* es.
Divine, *Divinus* i.
A Doctor, *Doctor* es.
A Dog, *Canis* es.
A Door, *Ostium* a.
Doun, *Lanugo* ines.
To draw, *Traho* ere.
A Drone, *Fucus* i.
Dry, *Aridus* i.
To dry, *Sicco* are.
To dy (by death) *Morior* i.
To dy (cloth) *Tingo* ere.
A Dyer, *Tinctor* es.

E.

A N Eagle, *Aquila* æ.
 An Ear, *Auris* es.
The Earth, *Terra* æ.
Eloquent, *Disertus* i.
An employment, *Occupatio* nes.
Empty, *Vacuus* i.
To encourage, *Foveo* ere.
To end, *Desino* ere.
To endure, *Patior* i.
An enemy, *Hostis* es.
An English, *Dictamen* ina.
Envy, *Invidia* æ.
Errour, *Error* ès.
An estate, *Census* ûs.
To exceed, *Supero* are.
To exercise, *Exerceo* ere.
To exhort, *Hortor* ari.
To expect, *Expecto* are.
To extinguish, *Extinguo* ere.
An Eye, *Oculus* i.

F 3   F. A

F.

A Face, *Facies ês.*
To fade, *Declino* are.
To fail, *Fruſtror* ari.
Fair, *Pulcher* ri.
Faithful, *Fidelis* es.
Fame, *Fama* æ.
Familiarity, *Familiaritas* tes.
A Farmer, *Colonus* i.
A Father, *Pater* tres.
A Fault, *Culpa* æ.
A fear, *Timor* es.
To fear, *Timeo* ere.
To feed, *Paſco* ere.
To fence, *Vallo* are.
A Fen, *Palus* ú des.
A Field, *Ager* gri.
To fight, *Pugno* are.
A File, *Lima* æ.
Filthy, *Turpis* es,
To finde, *Reperio* ire.
To fine, *Mulʈo* are.
To finiſh, *Abſolvo* ere.
A fire, *Ignis* es.
The Firmament, *Firmamentum* a.
Firme, *Firmus* i.
A Fiſh, *Piſcis* es.
To fit, *Apto* are.
To flee, *Fugio* ere.
To fleet, *Volito* are.
Fleeting, *Volucris* es.
To fly (haſten away, or avoid, *Fugio* ere, (of a Bird) *Volo* are.
To fling, *Calcitro* are.
A flock (of cattle) *Grex* ges, (of cloth) *Floccus* i.
To flow, *Fluo* ere.
A flower, *Flos* res.

A Fly, *Muſca* æ.
A Fold, *Ovile* ia.
To follow, *Sequor* i.
A fool, *Stultus* i.
A form, *Claſſis* es.
A Fort, *Propugnaculum* a.
Fortitude, *Fortitudo* ínes.
Foul, *Immundus* i.
To furbiſh, *Expolio* ire.
Freſh, *Frigidus* i.
To fret, *Corrodo* ere.
A friend, *Amicus* i.
A froſt, *Frigus* ora.
A fruit, *Fruĉtus* ûs.
Fulneſs, *Saturitas* tes.
A Fur, *Pellis* es.

G.

To gain, *Acquiro* ere.
A gale, *Aura* æ.
A Garden, *Hortus* i.
A Gardiner, *Hortulanus* i.
A Garland, *Corolla* æ.
A Garment, *Veſtis* es.
A Garret, *Cœnaculum* a.
A Gate, *Porta* æ.
To gather, *Colligo* ere.
A General, *Imperator* es.
To generate, *Gigno* ere.
Generous, *Generoſus* i.
Gentle, *Lenis* es.
To get, *Quæro* ere.
To give, *Do* are.
Glory, *Gloria* æ.
To glut, *Satio* are.
To go, *Incedo* ere.
A Graſhopper, *Cicada* æ.
Graſs, *Herba* æ.
A grate, *Clathrus* i.
To graſe, *Paſcor* i.

Greedineſs

Greediness, *Aviditas tes*.
To grieve (Act.) *Contristo are*.
  (Neut.) *Tristor ari*.
Grievous, *Gravis es*.
The ground, *Tellus ūres*.
To grow, *Cresco ere*.
A guard, *Satellitium a*.
A Gun, *Tormentum a*.

H.

A Hall, *Aula æ*.
  To handle, *Tracto are*.
Handsome, *Speciosus i*.
To hang (Act.) *Suspendo ere*.
  (Neut.) *Pendeo ere*.
A Harbor, *Portus ús*.
Hard, *Durus i*.
To harden, *Induro are*.
A Hare, *Lepus ōres*.
A Harvest, *Messis es*.
To haste or hasten, *Festino are*.
A Hatchet, *Securis es*.
A Hasel, *Corylus i*.
To hear, *Audio ire*.
The Heart, *Cor da*.
A Hearth, *Focus i*.
To heat (Act.) *Calfacio ere*.
  (Neut.) *Calesco ere*.
Heat, *Calor es*.
A Heath, *Ericetum a*.
Heavy, *Gravis es*.
A Hedge, *Sepis es*.
A Helm, *Clavus i*.
A help, *Subsidium a*.
An Herb, *Herba æ*.
To hew, *Cœdo ere*.
High, *Altus i*.
A Hill, *Collis es*.
A hindrance, *Impedimentum a*.
A Hoan, *Coticula æ*.

A Hodman, *Corbulo nes*.
Hollow, *Cavus i*.
Honest, *Probus i*.
Honey, *Mel la*.
Honor, *Honor es*.
Hope, *Spes ês*.
A Horn, *Cornu a*.
A Horse, *Equus i*.
A Horse-rider, *Eques ī:es*.
Hot, *Calidus i*.
A House, *Domus ûs*.
A House-keeper, *Dominus i*.
Huge, *Immanis es*.
Humility, *Submissio nes*.
Hunger, *Fames es*.
A Huntsman, *Venator es*.
A Hurdle, *Cratis es*.
A Husbandman, *Agricola æ*.
A Husk, *Siliqua æ*.

I.

Idle, *Ignavus i*.
Idleness, *Ignavia æ*.
Illustrious, *Illustris es*.
To inclose, *Circundo are*.
Industry, *Industria æ*.
Ingenious, *Ingeniosus i*.
An injury, *Injuria æ*.
Ink, *Atramentum a*.
To Inn, *Recondo ere*.
Joyful, *Lætus i*.
Iron, *Ferrum s*.
A Judge, *Judex ī:es*.
A Juyce, *Succus i*.
A Juncket, *Daps es*.
Just, *Justus i*.
Justice, *Justitia æ*.

K.

TO keep, *Cuſtodio* ire.
Kindneſs, *Humanitas* tes.
A King, *Rex* ges.
A Knife, *Culter* tri.
A Knot, *Nodus* i.
To know, *Scio* ire.

L.

LAbor, *Labor* es.
To labor, *Laboro* are.
A Laborer, *Operarius* i.
To laſt, *Duro* are.
Laughter, *Riſus* ûs.
A Law, *Lex* ges.
A Lawyer, *Cauſidicus* i.
Lazineſs, *Pigritia* æ.
To leap, *Salto* are.
Learning, *Doctrina* æ.
A Leſſon, *Lectio* nes.
A Letter, *Litera* æ.
Liberality, *Liberalitas* tes.
Life, *Vita* æ.
Light (Subſt.) *Lux* ces, (Adj.)
Levis es.
To like, *Probo* are.
A Lion, *Leo* nes.
A Liquor, *Liquor* es.
To load, *Onero* are.
Lofty, *Celſus* i.
Long, *Longus* i.
To looſe, *Perdo* ere.
A Lord, *Dominus* i.
Loſs, *Damnum* a.
To love, *Amo* are.
To loyter, *Ceſſo* are.
A Lute, *Cithera* æ.
Luxury, *Luxuria* æ.
To lye, *Faceo* ere.

M.

THe Magiſtrate, *Magiſtratus* ûs.
A Maid, *Ancilla* æ.
To make, *Facio* ere.
A Malefactor, *Reus* i.
Man, *Homo* ines.
To manage, *Rego* ere.
Many, *Multus* i.
To march, *Gradior* i.
A Marriner, *Nauta* æ.
Marrow, *Medulla* æ.
A Maſter (of Scholars) *Præceptor*
es, (of Servants) *Herus* i.
A Meadow, *Pratum* a.
Meal, *Farina* æ.
Meat, *Cibus* i.
A Medicine, *Pharmacum* a.
To mellow, *Miteſco* ere.
Melody, *Modulatio* nes.
To melt (Act.) *Liquefacio* ere.
(Neut.) *Liqueſco* ere.
A Merchant, *Mercator* es.
Mercy, *Miſericordia* æ.
Mildneſs, *Clementia* æ.
A Mill, *Molendinum* a.
A Miller, *Molitor* es.
A minde, *Mens* tes.
A Miſtreſs, *Hera* æ.
Moiſt, *Humidus* i.
To moiſten, *Humecto* are.
Moiſture, *Humor* es.
Mold, *Gleba* æ.
Money, *Pecunia* æ.
The Moon, *Luna* æ.
Mooriſh, *Uliginoſus* i.
The morning, *Aurora* æ.
A Mother, *Mater* tres.
Mountainy, *Montanus* i.

To

To mourn, *Mæreo ere.*
A Mower, *Messor es.*

N.

A Nail, *Vnguis es.*
Naked, *Nudus i.*
Nature, *Natura æ.*
Naughty, *Vitiosus i.*
A Needle, *Acus ûs.*
To neigh, *Hinnio ire.*
A Neighbor, *Vicinus i.*
A Nettle, *Vrtica æ.*
Niceness, *Fastidium a.*
Night, *Nox ctes.*
A Nurse, *Nutrix ices.*
A Nut, *Nux ces.*

O.

AN Oak, *Quercus ûs.*
Observance, *Observantia æ.*
To obtain, *Obtineo ere.*
An old Man, *Senex es.*
To oppress, *Opprimo ere.*
An Orator, *Orator es.*
An Ornament, *Ornamentum a.*
To over-cast, *Obduco ere.*
To over-come, *Vinco ere.*
An Ox, *Bos ves.*
An Oyster, *Ostreum a.*

P.

A Palace, *Palatium a.*
A Palm, *Palma æ.*
To Pamper, *Sagino are.*
To Pant, *Palpito are.*
Paper, *Charta æ.*
To pass, *Evado ere.*
A Pastor, *Pastor es.*

A Pasture, *Pascuum a.*
A Patient, *Æger gri.*
Pay, *Stipendium a.*
Peace, *Pax ces.*
A Peach, *Persicum a.*
A Pear, *Pyrum a.*
A Pen, *Penna æ.*
A Pen-knife, *Scalpellum a.*
A Penny, *As ses.*
A People, *Populus i.*
Perfume, *Suffimentum a.*
A Physician, *Medicus i.*
A Picture, *Pictura æ.*
A Pike, *Pilum a.*
A Pilot, *Nauclerus i.*
To pitch, *Furcillo are.*
A place, *Locus i (& a)*
To place, *Loco are.*
A Plain, *Campus i.*
To Plait, *Necto ere.*
To plant, *Planto are.*
To play, *Ludo ere.*
Play, *Lusus ûs.*
To plead, *Ago ere.*
A Pleader, *Actor es.*
Pleasant, *Jucundus i.*
Pleasure, *Voluptas tes.*
Plenty, *Copia æ.*
A Plombet, *Plumbeus i.*
To Plough, *Aro are.*
A Plough-man, *Arator es.*
A Poet, *Poeta æ.*
To Polish, *Polio ire.*
Poor, *Pauper es.*
A Porter, *Bajulus i.*
To possess, *Possideo ere.*
A Potion, *Potio nes.*
Poverty, *Paupertas tes.*
Practise, *Exercitatio nes.*
Practised, *Exercitatus i.*
Praise, *Laus des.*

To

To precede, *Præcedo* ere.
To prepare, *Paro* are.
To prescribe, *Præscribo* ere.
Pretious, *Pretiosus* i.
To prick, *Pungo* ere.
A prickle, *Sentis* es.
Pride, *Superbia* æ.
To print, *Imprimo* ere.
A Printer, *Typographus* i.
A prisoner, *Captivus* i.
A prize, *Palma* æ.
To produce, *Profero* re.
A Prong, *Bidens* tes.
A Prop, *Adminiculum* a.
To provide, *Paro* are.
Providence, *Frugalitas* tes.
Prudence, *Prudentia* æ.
To punish, *Punio* ire.
Punishment, *Pœna* æ.
A Puppy, *Catulus* i.
To purchase, *Acquiro* ere.
Purple, *Purpura* æ.
A Purse, *Crumena* æ.
To pursue, *Persequor* i.

Q.

A Queen, *Regina* æ.
Quick, *Agilis* es.
Quiet, *Tranquillus* i.
A Quiver, *Pharetra* æ.
To Quiver, *Tremo* ere.
Quivering, *Horridus* i,

R.

A Race, *Cursus* ûs.
To raise, *Erigo* ere.
A Rake, *Rastrum* (i &) a.
Rank, *Lætus* i.
A Rasor, *Novacula* æ.

To read, *Lego* ere.
To reap, *Meto* ere.
A Reaper, *Messor* es.
To recover, *Reduco* ere.
A Recreation, *Recreatio* nes.
Red, *Ruber* bri.
To reel, *Labo* are.
A refreshment, *Refectio* nes.
To rejoyce (Act.) *Lætifico* are,
   (Neut.) *Lætor* ari.
To relent, *Mollesco* ere.
To relieve, *Levo* are.
To remove, *Tollo* ere.
To repeat, *Repeto* ere.
To require, *Posco* ere.
Rest, *Quies* etes.
To restore, *Restituo* ere.
To restrain, *Arceo* ere.
To return, *Redeo* ire.
A reward, *Merces* edes.
Rich, *Opulentus* i.
To ride, *Equito* are.
To ring, *Tinnio* ire.
To rise, *Exto* are.
A River, *Amnis* es.
To rob (money) *Eripio* ere, (a
   person) *spolio* are.
To Roll, *Volvo* ere.
A Roof, *Tectum* a.
A Rose, *Rosa* æ.
To rot (Act.) *Putrefacio* ere,
   (Neut.) *Putresco* ere.
Rough, *Asper* i.
A Rower, *Remex* iges.
To Rule (Act.) *Rego* ere, (Pass)
   Regno are, (with a Ruler)
   Metor ari.
A Ruler, *Canon* ones.
To run, *Curro* ere.
To rush, *Ruo* ere.
Rust, *Rubigo* ines.

S. Sad

S.

SAd, *Triftis* es.
Safe, *Tutus* i.
A fafeguard, *Præfidium* a.
To fail, *Navigo* are.
A Sand, *Arena* æ.
A Saw, *Serra* æ.
A Sawyer, *Sector* es.
A Scabbard, *Vagina* æ.
To fcatter, *Spargo* ere.
A Scholar, *Scholaris* es.
A School *Schola* æ.
A School-fellow, *Condifcipulus* i.
A School-mafter, *Ludimagifter* ri.
A Scull, *Tefta* æ.
A Sea, *Mare* ia.
To fee, *Video* ere.
Seed-time, *Sementis* es.
To feek, *Quæro* ere.
To fell, *Vendo* ere.
A fent, *Odor* es.
A Servant, *Servus* i.
To fet, *Occido* ere.
Severity *Severitas* tes.
A fhadow, *Umbra* æ.
Sharp, *Acutus* i.
To fhave, *Rado* ere.
A Sheath, *Theca* æ.
A Sheep, *Ovis* es.
A Sheepfold, *Ovile* ia.
To fheer, *Tondeo* ere.
A fhell, *Tefta* æ.
A Shepherd, *Paftor* es.
A Sherman, *Pannitonfor* es.
A Ship, *Navis* es.
A Shore, *Littus* ora.
A Shower, *Imber* bres.
A Shrub, *Frutex* ices.
A Shuttle, *Radius* i.

A Sickle, *Falx* ces.
A fight, *Spectaculum* a.
To fing, *Cano* ere.
To fink (Act.) *Demergo* ere,
    (Neut.) *Subsido* ere.
Sinking, *Bibulus* i.
A Sifter, *Soror* es.
A Sithe, *Falx* ces.
To fit, *Sedeo* ere.
Skill, *Peritia* æ.
Skilful, *Peritus* i.
To fkip, *Salto* are.
Sleep, *Somnus* i.
Sloth, *Pigritia* æ.
A Smith, *Ferrarius* i.
A Snaffle, *Camus* i.
Soft, *Mollis* es.
To foften, *Mollio* ire.
Solid, *Solidus* i.
A Soldier, *Miles* ites.
To found, *Sono* are.
Sour, *Acerbus* i.
To fow (with thred) *Suo* ere,
    (Seed) *Sero* ere.
A Spade, *Ligo* nes.
Spatious, *Spatiofus* i.
To fpeak, *Loquor* i.
A fpice, *Aroma* ta.
To fpin, *Neo* ere.
A Spit, *Vern* a.
To fpred, *Expando* ere.
Spring (Adj.) *Vernus* i.
To fpring, *Virefco* ere.
A Spur, *Calcar* ia.
To fquare, *Quadro* are.
A Staff, *Baculus* i.
A Stag, *Cervus* i.
To ftain, *Maculo* are.
To ftand out, *Exto*, are.
Starry, *Stellatus* i.
To fteer, *Guberno* are.

To

To stick, *Hæreo* ere.
Stiff, *Rigidus* i.
To stile, *Appello* are.
The Stomack, *Appetitus* ûs.
A storm, *Procella* æ.
To stray, *Ruo* are.
A Street, *Compitum* a.
Strength, *Robur ora*.
To stretch, *Porrigo* ere.
Strong, *Validus* i.
Studious, *Studiosus* i.
To study, *Studeo* ere.
Success, *Successus* ûs.
Sullied, *Obsoletus* i.
Summer (Subst.) *Æstas* ātes,
   (Adject.) *Æstivus* i.
The Sun, *Sol* es.
Sure, *Certus* i.
To surround, *Ambio* ire.
To sustain, *Sustineo* ere.
A Swallow, *Hirundo* ìnes.
To swarm, *Ferveo* ere.
Sweet (in taste) *Dulcis* es, (in
   sent (*Suavis* es.
To swell, *Turgeo* ere.
Swift, *Pernix* ices.
To swim, *Nato* are.
A Sword, *Gladius* i.

T.

TO take, *Sumo* ere.
   To tame, *Domo* are.
A task, *Pensum* a.
A taste, *Sapor* es.
A Taylor, *Sartor* es.
To teach, *Doceo* ere.
Temperance, *Temperantia* æ.
A Tempest, *Tempestas* tes.
Tender, *Tener* i.
To thaw, *Solvo* ere.

Thick, *Densus* i.
A Thicket, *Fruticetum* a.
A Thief, *Fur* es.
To think, *Cogito* are.
A Thorn, *Rubus* i.
A thought, *Cogitatio* nes.
A Thred, *Filum* (i &) a.
A Threshold, *Limen ina*.
To Till, *Colo* ere.
Timber, *Materia* æ.
A Token, *Signum* a.
A Tongue, *Lingua* æ.
To tols, *Jacto* are.
A Tower, *Turris* es.
A Town-house, *Forum* a.
A Trade, *Ars* tes.
A Traveller, *Viator* es.
A Treasure, *Thesaurus* i.
A Tree, *Arbor* es.
A Truant, *Cessator* es.
To truant, *Cesso* are.
A Trumpet, *Tuba* æ.
To try, *Probo* are.
To tumble, *Ruo* ere.
Tunable, *Canorus* i.
To turn, *Verso* are.
To twitch, *Vellico* are.
To tye, *Vincio* ire.

V.

A Valley, *Vallis* es.
   Valor, *Virtus* tes.
Various, *Varius* i.
Vast, *Vastus* i.
Vehement, *Vehemens* tes.
A Vein, *Vena* æ.
Vertue, *Virtus ūtes*.
To vex, *Vexo* are.
Vice, *Vitium* a.
Vigilant, *Vigilans* tes.

A

A Village, *Villa* æ.
A Vine, *Vitis* es.
A Vineyard, *Vinea* æ.
A Violet, *Viola* æ.
Uncorrupt, *Incorruptus* i.
Unseasonable, *Intempestivus* i.
To unyoke, *Abjugo* are.
Use, *Confuetudo* ines.

W.

To wake (Act.) *Expergefacio* ere, (Neut.) *Vigilo* are.
To walk, *Ambulo* are.
A Wall (of a City) *Murus* i, (of a House) *Paries* etes.
To wander, *Vagor* ari.
Warm, *Apricus* i.
War, *Bellum* a.
Warfare, *Militia* æ.
To waste, *Confumor* i.
Water, *Aqua* æ.
To water, *Rigo* are.
Wax, *Cera* æ.
To wax, *Crefco* ere.
Wealth, *Opulentia* æ.
A Weapon, *Telum* a.
To wear, *Tero* ere.
Weather, *Tempestas* tes.
To weave, *Texo* ere.
A Weaver, *Textor* es.
Weeping, *Fletus* ûs.

A Well, *Puteus* i.
Welcome, *Gratus* i.
Wet, *Udus* i.
A Whale, *Balæna* æ.
Wheat, *Triticum.*
To whet, *Acuo* ere.
A Whet-stone, *Cos* tes.
To whisper, *Sufurro* are.
Wide, *Latus* i.
A Will, *Arbitrium* a.
The Wind, *Ventus* i.
A Window, *Fenestra* æ.
Wine, *Vinum* a.
Winter (Adj.) *Hybernus* i.
Wisdom, *Sapientia* æ.
To wither, *Marcefco* ere.
To be wont, *Soleo* ere.
A Wood, *Sylva* æ.
Wooll, *Lana* æ.
Work, *Opus* era.
To work (as Bees) *Mellifico* ari.
The World, *Orbis* es.
A Worm, *Vermis* es.
Wormwood, *Abfinthium* a.
Worthy, *Liberalis* es.
To write, *Scribo* ere.

Y.

Yarn, *Stamen* ina.
A Yoke, *Jugum* a.

F I N I S.

3 5282 00031 6888